Facilitator's Guide to Overcoming the Fear of Self-Promotion

Lead this Road-Tested Program for Your Clients, Students, or Book Group

Coach, teach, or facilitate self-employed professionals and creatives to promote themselves with confidence

C.J. Hayden

Wings for Business
Philadelphia, PA

Facilitator's Guide to Overcoming the Fear of Self-Promotion
Lead this Road-Tested Program
for Your Clients, Students, or Book Group
Copyright © 2025 C.J. Hayden

Published by Wings for Business
1500 Chestnut St, Ste 2 #1279 • Philadelphia, PA 19102
cjhayden.com

ISBN: 979-8-9990328-0-5

Contents

Introduction: What to Know Before You Begin

Who will benefit from this *Facilitator's Guide*

My book and program *Overcoming the Fear of Self-Promotion* is designed specifically for self-employed professionals and creatives—that valiant group of service providers who must market and sell their own services.

This *Facilitator's Guide* was written to provide coaches, counselors, trainers, facilitators, professional associations, training schools, employers, and book groups with a framework for using my *Overcoming Fear* program with their clients, students, members, employees, or reading group participants.

You'll need your own copy of the *Overcoming the Fear of Self-Promotion* book to make use of this *Facilitator's Guide,* and the folks who participate with you will each need their own copy of the *Overcoming Fear* book as well. The book is available from all major booksellers in both print and ebook formats and from cjhayden.com. You'll only need one copy of this *Facilitator's Guide,* just for yourself. If you're sharing or rotating leadership, you are welcome to share a single copy of the *Facilitator's Guide,* if you prefer.

With the help of this *Facilitator's Guide,* you'll be able to:

- Conduct a webinar, group coaching program, or workshop series based on the *Overcoming Fear* book

- Coach individual clients through the *Overcoming Fear* program

- Lead or co-lead a book discussion group, success team of your peers, or you and a buddy, who are working through the *Overcoming Fear* book together

Almost any self-employed professional or creative can benefit from the *Overcoming Fear* program. Some examples are: accountants, architects, artists, attorneys, bodyworkers, brokers of insurance or real estate, coaches, consultants, counselors, craftspeople, designers, engineers, financial advisors, freelancers, IT specialists, photographers, speakers, therapists, trainers, wellness practitioners, and writers.

If some of your potential participants don't fit into any of those categories—perhaps they own a business that sells products, they are jobseekers or students, or they are employees with no sales responsibilities—they may still find many of the *Overcoming Fear* techniques helpful to conquer their self-promotion fears.

Whether you're a coach or counselor who wants to help your self-employed clients build their confidence, a consultant or trainer who'd like to add the *Overcoming Fear* program to your portfolio, a professional association, employer, or training school leader who sees how your members, employees, or students could benefit from the *Overcoming Fear* program, or a reader of the book who wants companions to work through the book's exercises together, this *Facilitator's Guide* will provide you with everything you need.

How to use this *Facilitator's Guide*

The *Facilitator's Guide* is divided into six chapters following this one. Regardless of how you plan to use the *Overcoming Fear* program, you should read **Chapter One: How to Get Started**, **Chapter Two: Facilitating the Program for Groups or Individuals**, plus **Chapter Seven: Tips and Tricks for Leaders** and **Chapter Eight: How to Keep the Work Alive**.

Chapters Three through Six are dedicated to specific methods of marketing and delivering the *Overcoming Fear* program: public group programs, in-house group programs, book groups or peer success teams, and individuals. Once you decide how you plan to deliver the *Overcoming Fear* program, you can read only the chapter(s) relevant to the approach(es) you've selected. Chapter One will help you make that decision if you haven't already.

Because you are reading one book (this guide) and will be referring to another (the *Overcoming Fear* book), references in the following chapters to sections or pages from either book will each be prefaced with either *"Guide"* or *"Book,"* to make clear which book is being referenced.

By making use of this *Facilitator's Guide,* know that you'll be providing an important service. You'll be helping talented self-employed professionals and creatives work through their fear and resistance around self-promotion and become more courageous marketers. The participants you support in this way will then be able to bring more of their valuable services to the wider world. You'll be multiplying your own positive impact. Bravo!

Chapter One: How to Get Started

How the program works

The *Overcoming the Fear of Self-Promotion* program began as a workshop series I delivered to my own clients and students, both in person and virtually, in groups and one-on-one. The material in the program is based on research conducted by psychologists and neuroscientists, as well as my own decades of experience and training. It's been road-tested by hundreds of participants, whose feedback I incorporated into the program.

Now that the program is available as a book, self-employed professionals and creatives can read the material on their own and complete the skills practice exercises by themselves. And... that's nowhere near as powerful and effective as working through the *Overcoming Fear* book with the help of a coach, facilitator, buddy, or group.

This is where you come in. By leading others through the program, you'll be supplying them with **accountability**, **perspective**, and **support**.

- You'll provide **accountability** by assigning reading and exercises to be completed by a certain date. At times, you'll ask for participants to commit aloud to what they'll do. You'll also ask participants to report in about what they did and how it went for them. If you're delivering *Overcoming Fear* in a group setting, other participants will be holding each other accountable as well. This sort of "benevolent peer pressure" has proven to be highly effective at encouraging participants to fulfill their commitment to a program.

- Your participants will gain **perspective** from hearing about your personal experiences related to self-promotion, and in a group, how other participants respond to the principles and techniques they'll be learning. Discovering how others struggle with self-promotion will normalize your participants' own difficulties, helping to reduce any shame or inadequacy they feel. They'll benefit, too, from hearing about a variety of approaches and solutions.

- You'll also **support** your participants to get the most from the program and complete it successfully. Numerous exercises in the *Overcoming Fear* book require practice with another person or group, which you or other participants can provide. You may have specific expertise you can contribute, such as communication skills or coaching techniques. You'll provide your participants with a space for commiserating or celebrating to keep them moving forward.

We've all had the experience of buying a book or enrolling in a self-study program, then never completing it. The more challenging the content is, the more likely we are to put it aside. But when we enroll in a class, hire a coach, commit to a buddy, or join a group, we gain the accountability, perspective, and support to follow through on our intentions.

Your contribution as a coach, facilitator, or group leader is worthwhile and needed.

The Overcoming Fear program works well in three different settings:

1. A **group program** delivered by you, or you and a co-leader. It might be structured as a webinar series, live workshop series, or group coaching program. Your program might be an offering you sell to individuals or organizations, a no-cost opportunity you extend to prospective clients to gain their business, or a service you provide pro bono to a professional association or training school you support.

2. An **individual coaching** experience you provide to a client. This will typically be a service you charge for. You might structure it as a stand-alone coaching program or incorporate it into a coaching relationship that also encompasses other issues.

3. A **peer success team** (or pair of buddies) working through the program together. This may take the form of a book discussion group that meets regularly to practice the exercises and report on their experiences. Or it could be a special interest group or community of practice within an employer organization, training school, or professional association. There may be just one group leader, or members may take turns facilitating the sessions.

In any of these settings, the leader and participants may meet in person, online, or even by phone.

I don't recommend that you attempt to deliver the *Overcoming Fear* program all at once, as a one-time event. Participants need to practice the exercises over time—and in some cases, in real world environments—for them to gain the full benefit. *Overcoming Fear* is a highly experiential program, and your participants must have the opportunity to apply what they are learning.

Delivering the program works well in either a nine-session series or a five-session series, depending on the length of each session and how often they take place. Below is the content from the *Overcoming Fear* book I suggest you include in each session, shown for the two different formats.

In a nine-session series, meeting weekly:

- Session 1 | Kickoff
  Book Content—**What to Know Before You Begin** and **Chapter One: You Can Learn to Manage Fear**

- Session 2 | *Book* Content—**Chapter Two: Building Your Fear-Defeating Muscles**

- Session 3 | *Book* Content—**Chapter Three: Taming Your Inner Critic**

- Session 4 | *Book* Content—**Chapter Four: Identifying Your Self-Promotion Fears**

- Session 5 | *Book* Content—**Chapter Five: Finding Your Personal Fear Antidote**

- Session 6 | *Book* Content—**Chapter Six: Developing Your Fear Antidote**

- Session 7 | *Book* Content—**Chapter Seven: Quick Fixes for Fearful Moments**

- Session 8 | *Book* Content—**Chapter Eight: Defeating Fear with Stronger Relationships**

- Session 9 | Wrap-up
  Book Content—**What to Do When You Finish this Book**

With a nine-session series, an effective session length for a group program is one hour. Working with an individual, you can schedule a full hour for each session, shorten each session to forty-five minutes, or devote an appropriate time period to the *Overcoming Fear* work within a regular session. A nine-session series, meeting weekly, fits neatly into a two-month period.

In a five-session series, meeting biweekly or monthly:

- Session 1 | Kickoff
  Book Content—**What to Know Before You Begin** and **Chapter One: You Can Learn to Manage Fear**

- Session 2 | *Book* Content—**Chapter Two: Building Your Fear-Defeating Muscles** and **Chapter Three: Taming Your Inner Critic**

- Session 3 | *Book* Content—**Chapter Four: Identifying Your Self-Promotion Fears** and **Chapter Five: Finding Your Personal Fear Antidote**

- Session 4 | *Book* Content—**Chapter Six: Developing Your Fear Antidote** and **Chapter Seven: Quick Fixes for Fearful Moments**

- Session 5 | Wrap-up
  Book Content—**Chapter Eight: Defeating Fear with Stronger Relationships** and **What to Do When You Finish this Book**

For a five-session series, an effective session length for a group program is ninety minutes. Working with an individual, you can schedule an hour per session, or devote an appropriate time period to the *Overcoming Fear* work within a regular session. A five-session series, meeting biweekly, would fit into four months. Meeting monthly, a five-session series would require five months.

Any of these arrangements can be effective, so you're free to design your program how it will work best for you and the type of group or individual you plan to work with.

Where to begin

If you think you'd like to deliver *Overcoming Fear* to paying participants as a public or in-house group program, or as individual coaching, the first step I recommend you take is to read the *Overcoming Fear* book from cover to cover, if you haven't already. You need to be familiar enough with the book's content to answer questions about it from your potential participants, and to gain confidence that you can lead or co-lead the program.

In this situation, I suggest you work through the program yourself on your first reading, completing each exercise as you go. That way, you'll experience the *Overcoming Fear* book as an unaccompanied reader would. You'll be able to give your participants examples of where you got stuck working on your own, and share what you learned or felt along the way.

If your idea is to work through the *Overcoming Fear* program together with a group of peers or with a buddy, there's no need to read the whole *Overcoming Fear* book and complete the exercises before you get started. You may, however, wish to read the book's introduction and first chapter. That will likely give you enough background to confirm you'd like to go ahead with a buddy or peer success team, and recruit people to join you.

Once you've done the reading I suggest above, decide how you want to deliver the program, at least for now. Then follow the appropriate next steps below to get started.

For coaches, trainers, or facilitators leading group programs

The *Overcoming Fear* program works well as either a public program, in which participants enroll themselves, or as an in-house program, where a company or other organization provides the participants and compensates you for the whole group. The program is also ideal to offer through a professional association or training school, where the organization markets the program to their members or students, then shares a percentage of the enrollment fees with you.

To offer *Overcoming Fear* as a public program, you'll need to:

1. Choose an audience
2. Set your price and minimum enrollment
3. Design a marketing and sales campaign
4. Create promotional tools
5. Set up registration
6. Enroll participants

For more on each of the above steps, see *Guide* **Chapter Three: Marketing and Enrollment for Public Group Programs**.

To offer *Overcoming Fear* as an in-house program, you'll need to:

1. Choose a target market
2. Determine your price range and minimum enrollment
3. Design a marketing and sales campaign
4. Create marketing tools
5. Prepare a proposal for prospective sponsors
6. Close the sale

For more on each of the above steps, see *Guide* **Chapter Four: Marketing and Enrollment for In-House Group Programs**.

To offer *Overcoming Fear* as a book discussion group, peer success team, or with a buddy:

1. Choose an audience
2. Set your price (if any) and minimum enrollment
3. Set up any registration or payment
4. Design an enrollment campaign
5. Create promotional tools
6. Recruit participants

For more on each of the above steps, see *Guide* **Chapter Five: Facilitating Book Groups or Success Teams.**

For coaches working with individuals

To offer *Overcoming Fear* to your current clients, you'll need to:

1. Decide which clients would benefit
2. List talking points to bring up in a future coaching session
3. Agree with each client how to best integrate *Overcoming Fear* with their regular coaching

For more on each of the above steps, see *Guide* **Chapter Six: Coaching Individuals**.

To offer *Overcoming Fear* as a package to prospective clients, you'll need to:

1. Choose an audience
2. Establish your price and working arrangement
3. Create promotional tools
4. Include the program in your existing marketing and sales campaigns for coaching
5. Enroll participants

For more on each of the above steps, see *Guide* **Chapter Six: Coaching Individuals**.

Who are the best candidates to participate

Any self-employed professional or creative who personally offers a business-to-business (B2B) or business-to-consumer (B2C) service, or sells products they themselves have created—such as those professionals listed in the *Guide* **Introduction**—can potentially benefit from the *Overcoming Fear* program. Other likely candidates are professionals who are employed by an organization but are expected to build their own book of business, such as accountants, attorneys, financial advisors, and insurance or real estate brokers.

Professionals and creatives like those above often have little background or training in marketing and sales. Their expertise is in their professional specialty: law, coaching, art, accounting, therapy, design, bodywork, financial planning, etc.

Even professionals who have prior experience in marketing or selling can run into difficulty when they first begin to promote their own services. When it's your own business you need to talk up; when you're having one-on-one conversations with people who might say no; when you run the risk of your website, blog post, event listing, or paid ad being ignored or disparaged; it's fertile territory for fear, resistance, and the inner critic to take over.

Owners of product-based businesses and salespeople for larger companies can experience these obstacles, too, so there's no need to exclude them from participating in a program you lead. But for professionals who are marketing their own services, or creatives marketing their own work, when a prospective client or buyer ignores them or turns them down, the rejection feels *personal*. It can seem as if their very identity is being attacked or belittled.

That's why you'll find that self-employed professionals and creatives, plus employed professionals building a personal book of business, are the most likely candidates to spot the immediate value of participating in the *Overcoming Fear* program. The exercises and examples in the *Overcoming Fear* book are tailored specifically for this group.

This program doesn't replace therapy or counseling

One important note about choosing and working with your participants: *Overcoming Fear* is a coaching and training program; it's not a therapeutic process. The program is designed for people seeking to function at a higher level rather than those wanting to heal psychological dysfunction. The exercises work with a participant's conscious mind, teaching new skills and tools, and solving problems through action. If you encounter potential participants who seem to be seeking resolution and healing for childhood issues, emotional pain, or trauma, they may not be candidates for this program unless they are also working with a therapist or counselor.

If a potential participant—or one you're already working with—appears to be unlikely to benefit from the program's exercises, telling you they feel stuck, frozen, or terrified by negative emotions, consider this guideline from the International Coaching Federation (ICF): "The client may benefit from working with a mental health professional if the client raises issues that relate to a history of unresolved emotional issues preventing the client from moving forward or if current life circumstances are creating barriers for making progress in the coaching process for growth."

When you uncover issues like these blocking a current or potential participant, you may wish to have a private conversation in which you gently suggest they pursue alternatives other than your program or group. You'll find helpful guidelines for this type of conversation on the websites of The National Alliance on Mental Illness, nami.org, or Mental Health America, mhanational.org.

If you have questions about whether someone is an appropriate candidate for coaching, either before enrolling them or after your program is in progress, I suggest you read the ICF guide: "Hullinger, A. M. and DiGirolamo, J. A. (2018). Referring a client to therapy: A set of guidelines." It's available at no cost on their website, coachingfederation.org.

Guidelines for using the *Overcoming Fear* book

While this *Facilitator's Guide* will provide what you need to lead others through the *Overcoming Fear* program, you and every participant will each need your own copy of the *Overcoming Fear* book. Facilitators typically require each participant to purchase the book themselves, just as they might for a college course. The book is available in paperback and multiple ebook formats at most online booksellers, and cjhayden.com.

In addition, a set of companion slides for leading the program in group settings, plus many of the sample facilitator tools in the **Guide Appendix**, are available for you to download at no cost. Visit chayden.com/ofsp-leaders for these.

You are welcome to read aloud brief portions of either this *Facilitator's Guide* or the *Overcoming Fear* book when delivering the program. You're also welcome to record sessions of your programs for enrolled participants who miss a session or want to listen again later.

You don't, however, have permission to record an entire *Overcoming Fear* program for the purpose of making it available to those who aren't enrolled in a live program with you. Nor do you have permission to record or reproduce any content from the *Overcoming Fear* book, or the companion slides, for the purpose of sharing it with those who don't own the book already. Recording or reproduction of this material would be a violation of copyright law. Thank you for respecting my intellectual property.

With you as a facilitator, the *Overcoming Fear* program will be able to help even more self-employed professionals and creatives than before. Let's make it happen together!

Chapter Two: Facilitating the Program for Groups or Individuals

Overcoming Fear suits multiple program formats

You should read this chapter no matter how you plan to offer the *Overcoming Fear* program: whether to groups or individuals. Your program could be delivered by you alone, by you and a co-leader together, or with just you and a buddy. Your program might be structured as an online webinar series, an in-person workshop series, or a group coaching program offered online or in person.

Your program could be a public offering for which you charge a fee. You would enroll individual participants on your website, or via a ticketing platform like Eventbrite, or using an online payment system like PayPal. You might also offer *Overcoming Fear* as a no-cost opportunity you extend to prospective clients to gain their business.

Or, you might offer *Overcoming Fear* as an in-house training program to a company, nonprofit, professional association, or school. The organization would pay you directly for their employees, members, or students to participate. You could also offer *Overcoming Fear* as a pro bono service you provide to a professional association or training school you support.

Alternatively, you could offer *Overcoming Fear* to a book discussion group, a success team of peers wishing to work through the book together, or just for you and a buddy.

Finally, you may choose to offer *Overcoming Fear* only to individuals as a one-on-one coaching program. These individuals could be your existing coaching clients or new prospective clients to whom you offer the program.

Regardless of the program structure you elect, you can also choose whether to offer your program in person or online. Most facilitators prefer delivering programs online, via webinar, since the design of the *Overcoming Fear* program requires a series of several sessions. But you might prefer in-person meetings, which you could hold in a café, co-working space, or private office. With either an in-person or online setting, you may wish to record your sessions to allow participants who miss one to easily catch up.

In this chapter, you'll learn exactly how to facilitate *Overcoming Fear* for a group, buddy, or individual program. Following this chapter, you'll learn how to market your program to your chosen audience, and enroll your group's participants.

How many participants should a group program have?

For public or in-house programs, you can have a successful program with as few as two participants so long as they both commit to attend every session. If you're organizing a book group or peer success team, you can successfully operate an *Overcoming Fear* program with only one other participant besides yourself. For any group, however, more participants will create a more powerful and reliable experience for everyone.

A good minimum number to aim for is four participants total (three plus yourself for a book group/success team). That way, you'll still have interaction if one or two participants miss a session. Of course, if you're hoping to earn a profit from the program and your income depends on how many people enroll, you will likely wish to set a higher minimum. You'll find more about this topic in *Guide* **Chapter Three: Marketing and Enrollment for Public Group Programs** and *Guide* **Chapter Four: Marketing and Enrollment for In-House Group Programs**.

The maximum number of participants will depend on how many people the physical or virtual meeting space can accommodate and the facilitator can manage. For most inexperienced facilitators, a comfortable maximum would be ten. If you're an experienced facilitator, you could easily handle up to twenty. An even higher number of participants would be possible if you have the physical or virtual space to create breakout groups, so that everyone gets a chance to practice and share.

How to facilitate the program

Following are step-by-step instructions with a suggested timeline for leading your group, buddy, or client through the *Overcoming Fear* program. Instructions for delivering a nine-session program appear first, followed by instructions for a five-session series. The suggested timeline for each session includes a five-minute cushion to allow for the inevitable late start or tech issue.

Where learning points include references to the *Overcoming Fear* book, they are given by both page number for the print and PDF editions, and by section heading or text string for ebook editions, to facilitate using a search function to find them.

If you're planning to co-facilitate the program with another leader, or rotate the facilitator role, see the section "Facilitating with multiple leaders" at the end of this chapter.

When the outline describes conducting a breakout session, fishbowl session, or group debrief, refer to the *Guide* **Appendix** for more details about how to facilitate these.

Where the outline notes "Watch/listen for," you'll find possible solutions for many of these situations in *Guide* **Chapter Seven: Tips and Tricks for Leaders**. In some cases, simply telling a participant "I notice that you…" and telling them what you observed, may be all you need to say.

If you wish to use visuals to facilitate the program in a group setting, a set of companion slides, plus many of the sample facilitator tools in the *Guide* **Appendix**, are available for you to download at no cost. Visit chayden.com/ofsp-leaders for these.

Nine-Session Weekly Series—60 minutes per session

PRE-WORK—Assign reading of *Book* **What to Know Before You Begin** and *Book* **Chapter One: You Can Learn to Manage Fear**

SESSION 1—Kickoff: *Book* **What to Know Before You Begin** and *Book* **Chapter One: You Can Learn to Manage Fear**

» Introduce the program and participants (15 min)

- If you're recording, turn on your device!
- Welcome your participants and tell them you're excited to facilitate
- Describe the program's history to make it and you more credible [*Book* pg 1; "Where this book came from"]
- Tell them who the program is for, how it works, what they'll get [*Book* pgs 1-3; "What to Know Before You Begin"]
- Ask for agreement with a confidentiality pledge, such as: "Keep confidential whatever you learn about other participants. You are welcome to discuss your own learning and experience in the program, but no one else's."
- Establish ground rules for productive learning [*Guide* Appendix; "Sample program syllabus"]
- Ask each participant to briefly introduce themselves and state what they want to get from the program (with a large group, you may wish to do this in dyads or triads)
- Introduce yourself
- Explain any additional materials you're providing [*Guide* Chapter Two; "Optional participant materials"]
- Ask for questions/comments

- Watch/listen for anyone: With unrealistic expectations of what they'll get from the program

» Explain principles for learning and change (10 min)

- Assure them that confident self-promoters are made, not born [*Book* pg 5; "Confident self-promoters are made not born"]
- They're not the only ones who feel afraid [Book pg 7; "You are not the only one who feels afraid"]
- Tell a story of successfully overcoming fear [A story of your own, of a client, or *Book* pg 7; "You are not the only one who feels afraid"]
- The special aspect of self-promotion for self-employed folks [*Book* pg 8; "When you promote your business, you're promoting yourself]
- Ask for questions/comments

» Teach the I AAM Technique (10 min)

- Teach the I AAM Technique skill [*Book* pgs 10-11; "Managing Fear with the IAAM Technique"]
- Explain why it works, share the Eckhart Tolle quote, and give an example [*Book* pgs 12-13; "Why the IAAM Technique works" or share your own example]
- Ask for questions/comments

» Facilitate practice of the I AAM Technique (15 min)

- For groups: One or two fishbowl exercises with a volunteer, or small group breakout exercises, followed by a full group debrief about how the practice went
- For individuals and buddies: Practice and debrief with your client/buddy

- Watch/listen for anyone: Adding judgment or criticism to their awareness and acceptance

» **Conclude with homework and reminders (5 min)**

- Assign skills practice of the IAAM Technique [*Book* pg 16; "Try the IAAM Technique"] and reading of *Book* Chapter Two
- If you're offering the practice pal option, describe how to participate [*Guide* Chapter Two: "Organizing practice pals"] (You might need to allow an extra 5 minutes for this in your timeline)
- Remind them of the day/time for next session, and how to ask questions of you in between
- Share the Billie Jean King quote or another of your choice [*Book* pg 16; "Billie Jean King"]

SESSION 2—*Book* **Chapter Two: Building Your Fear-Defeating Muscles**

» **Discuss the homework (10 min)**

- If you're recording, turn on your device!
- Ask a participant to summarize the IAAM Technique [*Book* pg 10; "Managing Fear with the IAAM Technique"]
- Ask 1-3 participants to share what they experienced and learned using the IAAM Technique
- Answer any remaining questions from Session 1
- Watch/listen for anyone: Not yet understanding the IAAM Technique; adding judgment or criticism to their awareness and acceptance

» Explain principle of leaning on strengths (10 min)

- Ask one or more participants what judgments come up for them when self-promoting

- Remind them to accept what is so, without judgment or criticism, and substitute curiosity [*Book* pgs 17-18; "What's going on in your head?"]

- Tell a story about how to take who you are and make that work for you [A story of your own, of a client, or *Book* pg 18; "Lean on your strengths to overcome fear"]

- Ask for questions/comments

- Watch/listen for anyone: Not able to identify their strengths; not seeing how their strengths will help

» Teach the Practice Loop (10 min)

- Teach the Practice Loop skill [*Book* pgs 19-20; "Learning new habits with the Practice Loop"]

- Explain how it works, share the James Clear quote, and give an example [*Book* pgs 22-24; "How to make the Practice Loop work for you" or share your own example]

- Ask for questions/comments

» Facilitate practice of the Practice Loop (15 min)

- For groups: Fishbowl exercise with a volunteer practicing their self-introduction, followed by you debriefing the volunteer about how the practice went

- For individuals and buddies: Have your client/buddy practice their self-introduction and debrief with you

- Ask for questions/comments

- Watch/listen for anyone: Expecting immediate improvement from practicing

» Explain about fear hiding itself (5 min)

- Describe how fear can hide behind resistance, procrastination, and avoidance [*Book* pgs 25-26; "Fear can hide behind resistance, procrastination, and avoidance"]

- Give an example [*Book* pgs 25-26; "Fear can hide behind resistance, procrastination, and avoidance" or share your own example]

- Ask for questions/comments

» Conclude with homework and reminders (5 min)

- Assign Practice Loop skills practice [*Book* pg 26; "Make use of the Practice Loop"] and reading of *Book* Chapter Three

- Remind them of the day/time for next session, and how to ask questions of you in between

- If you're offering the practice pal option, remind them to meet with their pal

- Share the Seth Godin quote or another of your choice [*Book* pg 28; "Seth Godin"]

SESSION 3—*Book* **Chapter Three: Taming Your Inner Critic**

» Discuss the homework (10 min)

- If you're recording, turn on your device!

- Ask a participant to summarize the Practice Loop [*Book* pg 19; "Learning new habits with the Practice Loop"]

- Ask 1-3 participants to share what they experienced and learned using the Practice Loop

- Answer any remaining questions from Session 2

- Watch/listen for anyone: Expecting immediate improvement from practicing; not able to identify their strengths; not seeing how their strengths will help

» **Explain how the inner critic works (10 min)**

- Define the inner critic and describe its function [*Book* pgs 29-30; "How your critical inner voice works"]
- Ask 1-3 participants to share favorite phrases of their own critic
- Describe how managing the inner critic improves self-promotion [*Book* pgs 30-32; "How managing your inner critic improves self-promotion"]

» **Teach disputing your inner critic (15 min)**

- Teach the disputation skill [*Book* pgs 32-35; "Disputing your inner critic"]
- Describe how to work with the disputation steps [*Book* pgs 35-37; "How to work with the disputation steps"]
- Demonstrate with a participant how disputation can work
- Ask for questions/comments
- Watch/listen for anyone: Not yet able to see how to practice disputation

» **Teach tricks to get past the inner critic quickly (15 min)**

- Describe some quick fix tricks to get past the inner critic [*Book* pg 39; "Tricks to get past your inner critic quickly"]
- Ask participants to share their own quick fixes
- Remind them to keep practicing disputation as well
- Ask for questions/comments

- Watch/listen for anyone: Wanting to replace disputation with quick fixes permanently

» **Conclude with homework and reminders (5 min)**

- Assign skills practice of inner critic disputation and quick tricks [*Book* pgs 41-42; "Try out managing your inner critic with disputation and quick tricks"] and reading of *Book* Chapter Four

- Remind them of the day/time for next session, and how to ask questions of you in between

- If you're offering the practice pal option, remind them to meet with their pal

- Share the Elizabeth Gilbert quote or another of your choice [*Book* pg 41; "Elizabeth Gilbert"]

SESSION 4—*Book* **Chapter Four: Identifying Your Self-Promotion Fears**

» **Discuss the homework (10 min)**

- If you're recording, turn on your device!

- Ask a participant to summarize taming the inner critic [*Book* pgs 32-35 and pg 39; "Disputing your inner critic" and "Tricks to get past your inner critic quickly"]

- Ask 1-3 participants to share what they experienced and learned using disputation techniques and quick fixes

- Answer any remaining questions from Session 3

- Watch/listen for anyone: Not able to distinguish between the inner critic and true inner guidance; struggling with the practice of disputation; placing too much reliance on quick fixes

» Explain why you should get to know your fear (5 min)

- Describe how knowing your fear helps you overcome it [*Book* pgs 43-44; "Why you should get to know your fear"]

- Give an example of someone who overcame their fear [*Book* pgs 43-44; "Why you should get to know your fear" or share your own example]

» Teach how to identify the Seven Fears of Self-Promotion (15 min)

- Describe each of the Seven Fears, asking participants to listen for which fears they recognize [*Book* pgs 44-46; "Recognizing the Seven Fears of Self-Promotion"]

- Remind participants to name their fear without judgment or guilt about it [*Book* pg 47; "Recognizing the Seven Fears of Self-Promotion"]

- Ask for questions/comments

- Watch/listen for anyone: Not able to see themselves having any of the fears; sliding into a helpless/hopeless place while thinking about fear

» Demonstrate with a participant how to find your self-promotion fear—*you may skip this when working with an individual or buddy who already knows their primary self-promotion fear, or if everyone in your group is already sure* (10 min)

- Ask for a participant who isn't sure which fear is primary

- Have them share their self-introduction

- Coach them to discover which fear they experienced [*Book* pgs 48-51; "Discovering your primary self-promotion fear"]

» Teach other ways to discover your primary self-promotion fear (10 min)

- List ways of probing deeper to find self-promotion fear [*Book* pgs 48-51; "Discovering your primary self-promotion fear"]
- Ask participants to share their own ideas
- Ask for questions/comments
- Watch/listen for anyone: Not yet sure which fear is primary

» Conclude with homework and reminders (5 min)

- Assign skills practice of practicing self-promotion and identifying their fear [*Book* pgs 51-52; "Practice self-promotion and identify your fear"] and reading of *Book* Chapter Five
- Remind them of the day/time for next session, and how to ask questions of you in between
- If you're offering the practice pal option, remind them to meet with their pal
- Share the Eleanor Roosevelt quote or another of your choice [*Book* pg 53; "Eleanor Roosevelt"]

SESSION 5—*Book* **Chapter Five: Finding Your Personal Fear Antidote**

» Discuss the homework (10 min)

- If you're recording, turn on your device!
- Ask a participant to summarize identifying self-promotion fears [*Book* pgs 44-46; "Recognizing the Seven Fears of Self-Promotion" and 48-51; "Discovering your primary self-promotion fear"]
- Ask 1-3 participants to share what they experienced and learned about identifying their fears

- Answer any remaining questions from Session 4
- Watch/listen for anyone: Stuck in a helpless/hopeless place while thinking about fear

» **Explain how to manage your fear, you must make friends with it (10 min)**

- Describe how getting into alliance with fear helps you overcome it [*Book* pgs 56-59; "To manage your fear, make friends with it"]
- Give evidence that getting into alliance with fear works [*Book* pgs 59-60; "To manage your fear, make friends with it"]
- Ask for questions/comments
- Watch/listen for anyone: Resistant to making friends with their fear

» **Teach how to find your fear antidote (15 min)**

- Describe the suggested antidotes for each of the Seven Fears, asking participants to listen for an antidote for their own fear [*Book* pgs 60-63; "Find your fear antidote"]
- Give an example of how to work with an antidote [*Book* pgs 63-64; "How it can look to reassure your fear" or share your own example]
- Ask for questions/comments
- Watch/listen for anyone: Not sure any of the antidotes will work for them

» **Demonstrate with a participant working with a fear antidote (15 min)**

- Ask for a participant to identify their primary fear and name a potential antidote

- Coach them to visualize taking an action that would trigger their fear, and imagine stepping into that antidote [*Book* pgs 65-66; "Discover your best fear antidote"]
- Ask them to share the result and whether that antidote feels right

» **Conclude with homework and reminders (5 min)**

- Assign skills practice of discovering their best fear antidote [*Book* pgs 65-66; "Discover your best fear antidote"] and reading of *Book* Chapter Six
- Remind them of the day/time for next session, and how to ask questions of you in between
- If you're offering the practice pal option, remind them to meet with their pal
- Share the Dale Carnegie quote or another of your choice [*Book* pg 66; "Dale Carnegie"]

SESSION 6 — *Book* **Chapter Six: Developing Your Fear Antidote**

» **Discuss the homework (10 min)**

- If you're recording, turn on your device!
- Ask a participant to summarize discovering and working with a fear antidote [*Book* pgs 60-62; "Find your fear antidote" and pgs 65-66; "Discover your best fear antidote"]
- Ask 1-3 participants to share what they experienced choosing and stepping into their antidote
- Answer any remaining questions from Session 5
- Watch/listen for anyone: Still unclear on how to determine an antidote; expecting dramatic improvement from trying one briefly

» Explain how building up fear antidotes works (5 min)

- Describe how antidotes must be built up to work best [*Book* pg 67; "Manage your fear by building up its opposite"]
- Ask for questions/comments

» Suggest and brainstorm strategies for building up fear antidotes (35 min)

- Spending 4-5 minutes each on the seven different suggested antidotes, name a strategy for building each one: confidence, self-assurance, comfort, knowledge, belief in the possibility of success, belief that success is okay, and self-sufficiency [*Book* pgs 67-75; "How to develop the antidote of confidence"]
- Brainstorm with participants additional strategies for building each suggested antidote
- Ask for questions/comments
- Watch/listen for anyone: Still not sure what antidote will work for them

» Conclude with homework and reminders (5 min)

- Assign skills practice of developing their fear antidote [*Book* pgs 79-80; "Try on a strategy to develop your fear antidote"] and reading of *Book* Chapter Seven
- Remind them of the day/time for next session, and how to ask questions of you in between
- If you're offering the practice pal option, remind them to meet with their pal
- Share the Martin Luther King quote or another of your choice [*Book* pg 80; "Martin Luther King"]

SESSION 7—*Book* **Chapter Seven: Quick Fixes for Fearful Moments**

» **Discuss the homework (10 min)**

- If you're recording, turn on your device!
- Ask a participant to summarize how building up fear antidotes works [*Book* pg 67; "Manage your fear by building up its opposite"]
- Ask 1-3 participants to share what they experienced and learned trying on a strategy to build up their antidote
- Answer any remaining questions from Session 6
- Watch/listen for anyone: Still skeptical about using an antidote to counteract their fear

» **Explain why quick fixes are necessary and good (5 min)**

- Describe how it will take time to build up their fear antidotes, so meanwhile quick fixes will help [*Book* pg 81; "Building up your fear antidotes will take time and practice"]
- Note how quick fixes are training wheels, not crutches [*Book* pgs 81-82; "Building up your fear antidotes will take time and practice"]

» **Suggest and brainstorm quick fixes for fear (35 min)**

- Spending 5 minutes each on the five suggested quick fixes from the book, describe how they work: become a problem-solver; talk about your clients; be yourself, not a salesperson; find a less scary path; and play a different tune [*Book* pgs 82-92; "Become a problem-solver"]
- Brainstorm with participants additional ideas for quick fixes
- Ask for questions/comments

- Watch/listen for anyone: Who believes none of the quick fixes will work for them

» **Conclude with homework and reminders (5 min)**

- Assign skills practice of continuing to build their fear antidote and adding a quick fix [*Book* pgs 93-94; "Continue building your fear antidote and add a quick fix"] and reading of *Book* Chapter Eight
- Remind them of the day/time for next session, and how to ask questions of you in between
- If you're offering the practice pal option, remind them to meet with their pal
- Share the Rosa Parks quote or another of your choice [*Book* pg 94; "Rosa Parks"]

SESSION 8—*Book* **Chapter Eight: Defeating Fear with Stronger Relationships**

» **Discuss the homework (10 min)**

- If you're recording, turn on your device!
- Ask a participant to summarize what a quick fix is and why to use one [*Book* pgs 81-82; "Building up your fear antidotes will take time and practice"]
- Ask 1-3 participants to share what they experienced and learned when using quick fixes
- Answer any remaining questions from Session 7
- Watch/listen for anyone: Still skeptical about the usefulness of quick fixes

» **Explain how and why it works to focus on relationships rather than sales (10 min)**

- Describe how stronger relationships help to overcome fear [*Book* pgs 95-97; "Overcoming fear at a deeper level"]

- Give an example of how stronger relationships can help [*Book* pg 97; "Overcoming fear at a deeper level" or share your own example]

- Ask for questions/comments

» **Discuss where and how to begin relationships with prospective clients and referral sources (15 min)**

- Describe how events and communities can lead to building relationships and list some types of events and communities that can be productive for meeting people [*Book* pgs 98-100; "Building relationships with prospective clients"]

- List ways to continue relationship-building after meeting [*Book* pg 100; "Building relationships with prospective clients"]

- Ask participants for their own examples of relationship-building

» **Explain how to transcend barriers to relationship-building (5 min)**

- Describe how it works best to find natural ways to connect and people who are open to relationships [*Book* pgs 100-102; "Transcending barriers to relationship-building"]

- Ask for questions/comments

- Watch/listen for anyone: Not sure relationship-building will work for them

» Discuss where and how to begin relationships with supportive colleagues (10 min)

- Describe how building relationships with colleagues helps in overcoming fear [*Book* pgs 102-103; "Building relationships with supportive colleagues"]

- List some types of events and communities that can be productive for meeting colleagues [*Book* pg 103; "Building relationships with supportive colleagues"]

- Ask participants for their own examples of relationship-building with colleagues

- Watch/listen for anyone: Skeptical that colleagues will be supportive

» Conclude with homework and reminders (5 min)

- Assign skills practice of building more relationships [*Book* pgs 104-105; "Begin to build more relationships"] and reading of *Book* Chapter What to Do When You Finish this Book

- Ask participants to outline a personal fear management plan for themselves [*Book* pgs 107-109; "Put it all together and take it on the road"]

- Remind them of the day/time for next session, and how to ask questions of you in between

- If you're offering the practice pal option, remind them to meet with their pal

- Share the Erica Jong quote or another of your choice [*Book* pg 105; "Erica Jong"]

SESSION 9—Wrap-up: *Book* **What to Do When You Finish this Book**

» **Discuss the homework (10 min)**

- If you're recording, turn on your device!
- Ask a participant to summarize how relationship-building can help overcome fear [*Book* pgs 95-97; "Overcoming fear at a deeper level"]
- Ask 1-3 participants to share what they experienced and learned trying relationship-building
- Answer any remaining questions from Session 8
- Watch/listen for anyone: Still skeptical about the usefulness of relationship-building for them

» **Explain how to put together all the fear management strategies into a plan (10 min)**

- Describe the six steps for managing fear in the moment [*Book* pgs 107-108; "Put it all together and take it on the road"]
- Remind participants to also continue building relationships and building up their fear antidote [*Book* pgs 108-109; "Keep on building relationships and your fear antidote"]
- Ask for questions/comments

» **Invite participants to share their own fear management plan (25 min)**

- Model an example of what a fear management plan sounds like [*Guide* Appendix; "Sample participant's fear management plan"]
- Ask each participant to share their own plan

» **Conclude with thanks and next steps (10 min)**

- Thank and congratulate your participants for their participation and hard work

- Tell them how they can continue working with you and invite their interest [*Guide* Chapter Eight: How to Keep the Work Alive]

- Share the Louisa May Alcott quote or another of your choice [*Book* pg 109; "Louisa May Alcott"] plus any final words of your own

Five-Session Biweekly or Monthly Series—90 minutes per session

PRE-WORK—Assign reading of *Book* **What to Know Before You Begin** and *Book* **Chapter One: You Can Learn to Manage Fear**

SESSION 1—Kickoff: *Book* **What to Know Before You Begin** and *Book* **Chapter One: You Can Learn to Manage Fear**

» **Introduce the program and participants (15 min)**

- If you're recording, turn on your device!

- Welcome your participants and tell them you're excited to facilitate

- Describe the program's history to make it and you more credible [*Book* pg 1; "Where this book came from"]

- Tell them who the program is for, how it works, what they'll get [*Book* pgs 1-3; "What to Know Before You Begin"]

- Ask for agreement with a confidentiality pledge, such as: "Keep confidential whatever you learn about other participants. You are welcome to discuss your own learning and experience in the program, but no one else's."

- Establish ground rules for productive learning [*Guide* Appendix: "Sample program syllabus"]

- Ask each participant to briefly introduce themselves and state what they want to get from the program (with a large group, you may wish to do this in dyads or triads)

- Introduce yourself

- Explain any additional materials you're providing [*Guide* Chapter Two: "Optional participant materials"]

- Ask for questions/comments

- Watch/listen for anyone: With unrealistic expectations of what they'll get from the program

» Explain principles for learning and change (10 min)

- Assure them that confident self-promoters are made, not born [*Book* pg 5; "Confident self-promoters are made not born"]

- They're not the only ones who feel afraid [*Book* pg 7; "You are not the only one who feels afraid"]

- Tell a story of successfully overcoming fear [A story of your own, of a client, or *Book* pg 7; "You are not the only one who feels afraid"]

- The special aspect of self-promotion for self-employed folks [*Book* pg 8; "When you promote your business, you're promoting yourself]

- Ask for questions/comments

» Teach the I AAM Technique (10 min)

- Teach the I AAM Technique skill [*Book* pgs 10-11; "Managing Fear with the IAAM Technique"]

- Explain why it works, share the Eckhart Tolle quote, and give an example [*Book* pgs 12-13; "Why the IAAM Technique works" or share your own example]
- Ask for questions/comments

» **Facilitate practice of the I AAM Technique (15 min)**

- For groups: One or two fishbowl exercises with a volunteer, or small group breakout exercises, followed by a full group debrief about how the practice went
- For individuals and buddies: Practice and debrief with your client/buddy
- Watch/listen for anyone: Adding judgment or criticism to their awareness and acceptance

» **Conclude with homework and reminders (5 min)**

- Assign skills practice of the IAAM Technique [*Book* pg 16; "Try the IAAM Technique"] and reading of *Book* Chapters Two and Three
- If you're offering the practice pal option, describe how to participate [*Guide* Chapter Two: "Organizing practice pals"] (You might need to allow an extra 5 minutes for this in your timeline)
- Remind them of the day/time for next session, and how to ask questions of you in between
- Share the Billie Jean King quote or another of your choice [*Book* pg 16; "Billie Jean King"]

SESSION 2—*Book* **Chapter Two: Building Your Fear-Defeating Muscles** and *Book* **Chapter Three: Taming Your Inner Critic**

» **Discuss the homework (10 min)**

- If you're recording, turn on your device!
- Ask a participant to summarize the IAAM Technique [*Book* pg 10; "Managing Fear with the IAAM Technique"]
- Ask 1-2 participants to share what they experienced and learned using the IAAM Technique
- Answer any remaining questions from Session 1
- Watch/listen for anyone: Not yet understanding the IAAM Technique; adding judgment or criticism to their awareness and acceptance; expecting immediate improvement from practicing

» **Explain principle of leaning on strengths (5 min)**

- Remind participants of guideline to accept what is so, without judgment or criticism, and substitute curiosity [*Book* pgs 17-18; "What's going on in your head?"]
- Tell a story about how to take who you are and make that work for you [A story of your own, of a client, or *Book* pg 18; "Lean on your strengths to overcome fear"]
- Ask for questions/comments
- Watch/listen for anyone: Not able to identify their strengths; not seeing how their strengths will help

» **Teach the Practice Loop (10 min)**

- Teach the Practice Loop skill [*Book* pgs 19-20; "Learning new habits with the Practice Loop"]

- Explain how it works, share the James Clear quote, and give an example [*Book* pgs 22-24; "How to make the Practice Loop work for you" or share your own example]
- Ask for questions/comments

» **Facilitate practice of the Practice Loop (15 min)**

- For groups: Fishbowl exercise with a volunteer practicing their self-introduction, followed by you debriefing the volunteer about how the practice went
- For individuals and buddies: Have your client/buddy practice their self-introduction and debrief with you
- Ask for questions/comments
- Watch/listen for anyone: Expecting immediate improvement from practicing

» **Explain how the inner critic works (10 min)**

- Define the inner critic and describe its function [*Book* pgs 29-30; "How your critical inner voice works"]
- Ask 1-2 participants to share favorite phrases of their own critic
- Describe how managing the inner critic improves self-promotion [*Book* pgs 30-32; "How managing your inner critic improves self-promotion"]

» **Teach disputing your inner critic (15 min)**

- Teach the disputation skill [*Book* pgs 32-35; "Disputing your inner critic"]
- Describe how to work with the disputation steps [*Book* pgs 35-37; "How to work with the disputation steps"]
- Demonstrate with a participant how disputation can work
- Ask for questions/comments

- Watch/listen for anyone: Not yet able to see how to practice disputation

» **Teach skills to get past the inner critic quickly (15 min)**

- Describe some quick fix tricks to get past the inner critic [*Book* pg 39; "Tricks to get past your inner critic quickly"]
- Ask participants to share their own quick fixes
- Remind them to keep practicing disputation as well
- Ask for questions/comments
- Watch/listen for anyone: Wanting to replace disputation with quick fixes permanently

» **Conclude with homework and reminders (5 min)**

- Assign skills practice of the Practice Loop [*Book* pg 26; "Make use of the Practice Loop"] and inner critic disputation and quick tricks [*Book* pgs 41-42; "Try out managing your inner critic with disputation and quick tricks"] and reading of *Book* Chapters Four and Five
- Remind them of the day/time for next session, and how to ask questions of you in between
- If you're offering the practice pal option, remind them to meet with their pal
- Share the Elizabeth Gilbert quote or another of your choice [*Book* pg 41; "Elizabeth Gilbert"]

SESSION 3—*Book* **Chapter Four: Identifying Your Self-Promotion Fears** and *Book* **Chapter Five: Finding Your Personal Fear Antidote**

» Discuss the homework (10 min)

- If you're recording, turn on your device!
- Ask a participant to summarize the Practice Loop [*Book* pg 19; "Learning new habits with the Practice Loop"]
- Ask 1-2 participants to share what they experienced and learned using the Practice Loop
- Ask a participant to summarize taming the inner critic [*Book* pgs 32-35; "Disputing your inner critic" and pg 39; "Tricks to get past your inner critic quickly"]
- Ask 1-2 participants to share what they experienced and learned using disputation techniques and quick fixes
- Answer any remaining questions from Session 2
- Watch/listen for anyone: Expecting immediate improvement from practicing; not able to distinguish between the inner critic and true inner guidance; struggling with the practice of disputation

» Explain why you should get to know your fear (5 min)

- Describe how knowing your fear helps you overcome it [*Book* pgs 43-44; "Why you should get to know your fear"]
- Give an example of someone who overcame their fear [*Book* pgs 43-44; "Why you should get to know your fear" or share your own example]

» **Teach how to identify the Seven Fears of Self-Promotion (15 min)**

- Describe each of the Seven Fears, asking participants to listen for which fears they recognize [*Book* pgs 44-46; "Recognizing the Seven Fears of Self-Promotion"]

- Remind participants to name their fear without judgment or guilt about it [*Book* pg 47; "Recognizing the Seven Fears of Self-Promotion"]

- Ask for questions/comments

- Watch/listen for anyone: Not able to see themselves having any of the fears; sliding into a helpless/hopeless place while thinking about fear

» **Demonstrate with a participant how to find your self-promotion fear**—*you may skip this when working with an individual or buddy who already knows their primary self-promotion fear, or if everyone in your group is already sure* **(10 min)**

- Ask for a participant who isn't sure which fear is primary

- Have them share their self-introduction

- Coach them to discover which fear they experienced [*Book* pgs 48-51; "Discovering your primary self-promotion fear"]

» **Teach other ways to discover your primary self-promotion fear (10 min)**

- List ways of probing deeper to find self-promotion fear [*Book* pgs 48-51; "Discovering your primary self-promotion fear"]

- Ask participants to share their own ideas

- Ask for questions/comments

- Watch/listen for anyone: Not yet sure which fear is primary

» Explain how to manage your fear, you must make friends with it (5 min)

- Describe how getting into alliance with fear helps you overcome it [*Book* pgs 56-59; "To manage your fear, make friends with it"]

- Give evidence that getting into alliance with fear works [*Book* pgs 59-60; "To manage your fear, make friends with it"]

» Teach how to find your fear antidote (15 min)

- Describe the suggested antidotes for each of the Seven Fears, asking participants to listen for an antidote for their own fear [*Book* pgs 60-63; "Find your fear antidote"]

- Give an example of how to work with an antidote [*Book* pgs 63-64; "How it can look to reassure your fear" or share your own example]

- Ask for questions/comments

- Watch/listen for anyone: Not sure any of the antidotes will work for them

» Demonstrate with a participant working with a fear antidote (10 min)

- Ask for a participant to identify their primary fear and name a potential antidote

- Coach them to visualize taking an action that would trigger their fear, and imagine stepping into that antidote [*Book* pgs 65-66; "Discover your best fear antidote"]

- Ask them to share the result and whether that antidote feels right

» **Conclude with homework and reminders (5 min)**

- Assign skills practice of practicing self-promotion and identifying their fear [*Book* pgs 51-52; "Practice self-promotion and identify your fear"] and discovering their best fear antidote [*Book* pgs 65-66; "Discover your best fear antidote"] plus reading of *Book* Chapters Six and Seven

- Remind them of the day/time for next session, and how to ask questions of you in between

- If you're offering the practice pal option, remind them to meet with their pal

- Share the Dale Carnegie quote or another of your choice [*Book* pg 66; "Dale Carnegie"]

SESSION 4—*Book* **Chapter Six: Developing Your Fear Antidote and *Book* Chapter Seven: Quick Fixes for Fearful Moments**

» **Discuss the homework (10 min)**

- If you're recording, turn on your device!

- Ask a participant to summarize identifying self-promotion fears [*Book* pgs 44-46; "Recognizing the Seven Fears of Self-Promotion" and 48-51; "Discovering your primary self-promotion fear"]

- Ask 1-2 participants to share what they experienced and learned about identifying their fears

- Ask a participant to summarize discovering and working with a fear antidote [*Book* pgs 60-62; "Find your fear antidote" and pgs 65-66; "Discover your best fear antidote"]

- Ask 1-2 participants to share what they experienced choosing and stepping into their antidote

- Answer any remaining questions from Session 3

- Watch/listen for anyone: Stuck in a helpless/hopeless place while thinking about fear; still unclear on how to determine an antidote; expecting dramatic improvement from trying one briefly

» **Suggest and brainstorm strategies for building up fear antidotes (35 min)**

- Spending 4-5 minutes each on the seven different suggested antidotes, name a strategy for building each one: confidence, self-assurance, comfort, knowledge, belief in the possibility of success, belief that success is okay, and self-sufficiency [*Book* pgs 67-75; "How to develop the antidote of confidence"]

- Brainstorm with participants additional strategies for building each suggested antidote

- Ask for questions/comments

- Watch/listen for anyone: Still not sure what antidote will work for them

» **Explain why quick fixes are necessary and good (5 min)**

- Describe how it will take time to build up their fear antidotes, so meanwhile quick fixes will help [*Book* pg 81; "Building up your fear antidotes will take time and practice"]

- Note how quick fixes are training wheels, not crutches [*Book* pgs 81-82; "Building up your fear antidotes will take time and practice"]

» **Suggest and brainstorm quick fixes for fear (30 min)**

- Spending 4-5 minutes each on the five suggested quick fixes from the book, describe how they work: become a problem-solver; talk about your clients; be yourself, not a salesperson;

find a less scary path; and play a different tune [*Book* pgs 82-92; "Become a problem-solver"]

- Brainstorm with participants additional ideas for quick fixes
- Ask for questions/comments
- Watch/listen for anyone: Who believes none of the quick fixes will work for them

» **Conclude with homework and reminders (5 min)**

- Assign skills practice of developing their fear antidote [*Book* pgs 79-80; "Try on a strategy to develop your fear antidote"] and adding a quick fix [*Book* pgs 93-94; "Continue building your fear antidote and add a quick fix"], plus reading of *Book* Chapters Eight and What to Do When You Finish this Book
- Remind them of the day/time for next session, and how to ask questions of you in between
- If you're offering the practice pal option, remind them to meet with their pal
- Share the Rosa Parks quote or another of your choice [*Book* pg 94; "Rosa Parks"]

SESSION 5—Wrap-up: *Book* **Chapter Eight: Defeating Fear with Stronger Relationships** and *Book* **chapter What to Do When You Finish this Book**

» **Discuss the homework (10 min)**

- If you're recording, turn on your device!
- Ask a participant to summarize how building up fear antidotes works [*Book* pg 67; "Manage your fear by building up its opposite"]

- Ask 1-2 participants to share what they experienced and learned trying on a strategy to build up their antidote
- Ask a participant to summarize what a quick fix is and why to use one [*Book* pgs 81-82; "Building up your fear antidotes will take time and practice"]
- Ask 1-2 participants to share what they experienced and learned when using quick fixes
- Answer any remaining questions from Session 4
- Watch/listen for anyone: Still skeptical about using an antidote to counteract their fear or about the usefulness of quick fixes

» Explain how and why it works to focus on relationships rather than sales (10 min)

- Describe how stronger relationships help to overcome fear [*Book* pgs 95-97; "Overcoming fear at a deeper level"]
- Give an example of how stronger relationships can help [*Book* pg 97; "Overcoming fear at a deeper level" or share your own example]
- Ask for questions/comments

» Discuss where and how to begin relationships with prospective clients and referral sources (15 min)

- Describe how events and communities can lead to building relationships and list some types of events and communities that can be productive for meeting people [*Book* pgs 98-100; "Building relationships with prospective clients"]
- List ways to continue relationship-building after meeting [*Book* pg 100; "Building relationships with prospective clients"]
- Ask participants for their own examples of relationship-building

» Explain how to transcend barriers to relationship-building (5 min)

- Describe how it works best to find natural ways to connect and people who are open to relationships [*Book* pgs 100-102; "Transcending barriers to relationship-building"]
- Ask for questions/comments
- Watch/listen for anyone: Not sure relationship-building will work for them

» Discuss where and how to begin relationships with supportive colleagues (10 min)

- Describe how building relationships with colleagues helps in overcoming fear [*Book* pgs 102-103; "Building relationships with supportive colleagues"]
- List some types of events and communities that can be productive for meeting colleagues [*Book* pg 103; "Building relationships with supportive colleagues"]
- Ask participants for their own examples of relationship-building with colleagues
- Watch/listen for anyone: Skeptical that colleagues will be supportive

» Explain how to put together all the fear management strategies into a plan (10 min)

- Describe the six steps for managing fear in the moment [*Book* pgs 107-108; "Put it all together and take it on the road"]
- Remind participants to also continue building relationships and building up their fear antidote [*Book* pgs 108-109; "Keep on building relationships and your fear antidote"]
- Ask for questions/comments

» Invite participants to share their own fear management plan (15 min)

- Model an example of what a fear management plan sounds like [*Guide* Appendix; "Sample participant's fear management plan"]

- Ask each participant to share a first draft of their own plan

» Conclude with thanks and next steps (10 min)

- Thank and congratulate your participants for their participation and hard work

- Tell them how they can continue working with you and invite their interest [*Guide* Chapter Eight: How to Keep the Work Alive]

- Share the Louisa May Alcott quote or another you choose [*Book* pg 109; "Louisa May Alcott"], plus any final words of your own

Facilitating with multiple leaders

You may wish to share the facilitation role with another leader or leaders. Perhaps you have a colleague you will partner with to offer the program, or you'll be offering a book group or success team where members will take turns at leading.

The easiest way to share leadership is to have each leader facilitate a particular session. Before you begin a co-facilitated program, you and your colleague should decide between you which session each person will lead.

With a rotating leadership program, it's best to assign leadership roles before your first meeting, rather than take up session time deciding this. It's also recommended that you have a backup leader designated for each session in case the intended leader is absent.

In either case, be sure to communicate to your participants in advance who will be leading each session.

While it's possible to switch leaders within a session, or to have two people co-lead simultaneously, these approaches to leading require advanced facilitation skills that are outside the scope of this *Guide*.

Facilitating with a buddy

When there are just two of you working through the book together, it may not be necessary to designate who is "leading" at any specific time. You could simply use the guidelines for facilitation above while both of you follow along.

However, you might find it more effective to assign a leader for each session anyway. You may both find yourselves taking the program more seriously when you have a designated leader responsible for making sure that all key learning points are covered and assigned exercises are conducted.

Organizing practice pals

Providing participants with practice pals during the weeks of the program will make it easier for everyone to complete the skills practice you'll be assigning as homework, plus furnish your participants with additional accountability outside of class.

The best way to set up practice pals is for you to create a roster of all your participants and assign each person a practice pal to work with in between each of the program sessions. Because it could happen that any one participant might be a less-than-adequate practice pal, rotating pals for each practice session will provide your participants with the most satisfying experience.

Below is an example of how you could assign practice pals for a ten-participant group that will follow the five-session outline. You'll have one practice session between each program session, so you'll need to assign unique pals for four different practice sessions. Divide your participants into two equal-sized groups. Make a table listing your participants like the one below, and fill in the session numbers in any sequence that makes sense to you, such that each person only has one practice pal from the other group for each practice session.

	Rosa	Marty	Therese	Grace	Tim
Walt	Session 1	Session 2	Session 3	Session 4	
Monica		Session 1	Session 2	Session 3	Session 4
Aziz	Session 4		Session 1	Session 2	Session 3
Karola	Session 3	Session 4		Session 1	Session 2
Sean	Session 2	Session 3	Session 4		Session 1

If you happen to have an odd number of participants, create one trio for each practice session. Begin by assigning duos for each session, as above. Then find which participants in your chart have open sessions, and assign them to a duo for each missing session. Try not to assign any one person to a trio too often, but it may not be possible to have each person be in only one trio for the whole program, depending on the math. Below is an example.

Step 1: Participant duos

	Rosa	Marty	Therese	Grace	Tim	Mariko
Walt	Sess 1	Sess 2	Sess 3	Sess 4		
Monica		Sess 1	Sess 2	Sess 3	Sess 4	
Aziz			Sess 1	Sess 2	Sess 3	Sess 4
Karola	Sess 4			Sess 1	Sess 2	Sess 3
Sean	Sess 3	Sess 4			Sess 1	Sess 2

Step 2: Participant trios

Session 1: Mariko joins Sean and Tim

Session 2: Rosa joins Monica and Therese

Session 3: Marty joins Karola and Mariko

Session 4: Therese joins Walt and Grace

Provide your participants with a roster including everyone's contact information (both emails and mobile numbers are best), and ask them to reach out to all their practice pals immediately after the first session to propose a 30- to 45-minute practice time between the meeting time of each session. Duos should need only 30 minutes; trios may need 45 minutes. Advise them that locking in their practice schedule for the entire program during the first week is the best approach to make sure that all practice sessions happen. If a participant happens to miss a class session, they should still attend the following practice session whenever possible.

In each practice, duos and trios should have each participant take a turn at practicing the homework given for the previous session. For example, after Session 1, they would practice using the IAAM Technique from *Book* **Chapter One**.

Explain that while a practice pal is speaking, the other pal(s) should listen carefully and note what they hear. Then they should provide feedback using the "sandwich" approach, structured like this:

1. What I thought worked well was…

2. What I thought didn't work as well was…

3. What I appreciated was…

For example, a practice pal listening to someone's practice of the I AAM Technique might say:

1. I thought you did an excellent job of noticing what was going on with you about that thing.

2. What didn't work as well was that you didn't seem to accept everything you were noticing.

3. What I appreciated was your willingness to look honestly at this uncomfortable stuff.

Finally, remind participants of their confidentiality pledge, and that anything revealed by pals in practice sessions should not be discussed with others not enrolled in the program.

Optional participant materials

The content of the *Overcoming Fear* program is fully contained in the *Book*, but you may wish to provide your participants with some additional materials to enhance their experience. You or your program sponsor will want to send a welcome email (further described in *Guide* **Chapters Three, Four**, and **Five**), as well as reminder emails before each session, described below. You may also wish to provide the following as a separate document or documents:

- Syllabus for the program, including your ground rules for participants, the schedule of meetings for the program, required reading for each session, and suggested skills practice (see the *Guide* **Appendix** for a sample syllabus)

- Roster of all participants (this is a must if you're offering the practice pal option, but you may wish to provide it anyway)

- Practice pal assignments (if you're offering the practice pal option, you'll need to provide this)

While you could include all of this detail in the body of your welcome email, some folks don't have a good system for keeping track of important emails. If you instead provide this information in one or more PDFs, you can attach them to an email (or several emails) so that participants can download and store them, or even print them if that works better for the participant. You can also upload them to a cloud storage provider like Dropbox, OneDrive, Google Drive, or iCloud, so you can share them via links. When offering an in-person program, you can provide printed copies of these optional documents at the first meeting.

Sending recap and reminder emails

Immediately after delivering each session of the program, I recommend you send a recap email to all participants, summarizing:

- What was covered in the session

- How to catch up if they missed the session

- What the homework assignment is

- What they should address during practice pal sessions (if you're including this)

- Any preparation they should complete before the next session (such as reading a *Book* chapter)

- Day, time, and leader for the next session

Twenty-four hours before the next session, I suggest you send a reminder email to everyone, covering:

- What the homework and practice pal assignments were

- Any preparation they should complete before the session

- Day, time, and leader for the session

- Location and/or access information for the session

- How to contact the leader for questions or to let the leader know a participant will be absent

Your next steps

Now that you know more about the program you'll be leading, you're ready to start marketing your program and enrolling participants. If you plan to offer *Overcoming Fear* as a group program to a public audience you recruit yourself, refer to **Guide Chapter Three: Marketing and Enrollment for Public Group Programs**. If instead you'll be offering an in-house group sponsored by an organization, you can skip *Guide* Chapter Three, and refer to ***Guide*** **Chapter Four: Marketing and Enrollment for In-House Group Programs**. And if you will offer the program as a book discussion group or peer success team, refer to ***Guide*** **Chapter Five: Marketing and Enrollment for Book Groups or Success Teams**.

Note that if you plan to work through the *Overcoming Fear* program with just you and a buddy, and already have a buddy lined up, you can skip the marketing and enrollment chapters and return to the section "How to facilitate the program" in this chapter when you're ready to get started. If you haven't yet found a buddy to work with, you'll find help in ***Guide*** **Chapter Five: Marketing and Enrollment for Book Groups or Success Teams**.

Chapter Three: Marketing and Enrollment for Public Group Programs

Who should read this chapter

In this chapter, you'll find guidelines for marketing a public group program—that is, a group program that you market to individuals who don't necessarily know each other, and who will enroll themselves. If instead, you wish to offer *Overcoming Fear* as an in-house program to an organization, or as a book group or peer success team, you should read *Guide* **Chapter Four: Marketing and Enrollment for In-House Programs** or *Guide* **Chapter Five: Marketing and Enrollment for Book Groups or Success Teams**.

Choose an audience or target market

Your first necessary step will be to decide what audience of individuals you wish to target. You'll find a description of the best candidates for the program in the section "Who are the best candidates to participate" in *Guide* **Chapter One**.

While you can certainly offer your program to anyone who might benefit, you'll have more success when you focus on an audience you already know or have connections to. This is particularly true when you're just getting started promoting your program.

Consider how much more attractive a program called "Life Coaches: Overcome the Fear of Self-Promotion" would be to those coaches than the more anonymous "Overcome the Fear of Self-Promotion." Or, the attractiveness of "Fearless Self-Promotion for Attorneys" or "Designers: You Can Conquer the Fear of Self-Promotion" to those specific groups.

Yes, you are limiting your reach by pursuing a particular audience, but you are also giving yourself the ability to target that group more directly. And, once that group learns of your program, they will be more attracted to it. So, do consider choosing an audience you have a strong affinity with and already have some connections to.

Your audience could be local, regional, national, or international, depending on your own existing reach and preferences. If you choose a local audience, you could potentially offer your programs in person. But since the design of the *Overcoming Fear* program requires a series of sessions rather than a one-time meeting, most facilitators prefer to deliver their programs online, via webinar.

You're welcome to position your program as a "course," "class," "webinar series," "coaching program," or apply any other descriptive label that seems right for you and your audience.

Set your price and minimum enrollment

Before offering your program, you'll need to determine what price would be attractive to your audience and fair to you. You may consider offering your program at no cost as a method of attracting new clients, but I recommend you charge at least a nominal amount to pre-screen your participants as people who are willing to pay something for your services. Paying a fee to enroll also encourages more participation than when participants can attend for free.

The best way to approach setting your price is to first consider the total amount you need to walk away with for this program to be worth your while. Let's say you'd like to earn at least $2,000 for your program, and you have no additional costs to cover. If you could attract eight participants, that would mean each person would need to pay at least $250 ($2,000 ÷ 8).

That $250 price would be just the minimum to meet your earnings target in this example; it's not a recommendation. You can charge as much as you believe your participants will pay. The more tailored your program is to your audience, the higher the acceptable price is likely to be.

Whatever price you choose, decide before you begin to market what minimum number of participants you will need to make running your program worthwhile. As the start date approaches, you can decide whether you have enough people to go forward, or if you should delay, cancel, or employ emergency enrollment methods. (See "Emergency enrollment measures" in the *Guide* **Appendix** for more.)

Set up registration and payment

You'll need a method for participants to enroll themselves and pay you. Ideally, the platform you use will also deliver to your participants a welcome letter with information about the program. Here are some options you might consider:

- A page on your own website enabled for payment with a shopping cart like Shopify or WooCommerce.

- A page on your own website enabled for payment with a third-party provider like PayPal or Stripe. Note that these options can limit your ability to deliver immediate welcome emails without an add-on service.

- A page on an event platform that accepts registration payments, such as Eventbrite or Meetup.

I don't recommend accepting payment in any way that requires participants to leave your registration page in order to register, such as asking them to pay you separately via PayPal or Venmo. Adding this extra step creates an extra level of difficulty and inconvenience that will reduce your enrollments.

Design a marketing and sales campaign

You'll need a marketing and sales campaign to successfully promote your program. You should plan to begin promoting your program six weeks before you intend the program to begin.

In addition to any regular marketing you do for your business, activities like those described below will help you create a campaign specifically for your *Overcoming Fear* programs. Here are some of the promotional strategies you should consider:

- Web page—Add a page about the program to your existing website, set up a standalone site for just this program, or create a page on an event platform that accepts registration payments, such as Eventbrite or Meetup.

- Broadcast email—Send a series of emails to your existing mailing list, or assemble a new mailing list for this program.

- Social media—Make text or video posts about the program periodically, leading up to the program date.

- Event listings—Create listings for the program on event calendars in addition to the platform where you're taking registrations. Consider general calendars like those on Facebook or LinkedIn, as well as others specific to your target audience or geographic area.

- Flyer/promo card distribution—Make flyers or promo cards available at events you're attending, and venues that attract your target audience.

- Networking groups and events—Participate in groups and events where you can network with other attendees, seeking out groups and events that will attract potential participants. Consider both in-person and virtual groups and events, which you might find on LinkedIn, Facebook, Meetup, Eventbrite, and other platforms specific to your locale or audience.

- Personal follow-up—Send personal emails or texts, or make follow-up phone calls, to people you believe are interested in the program.

- Blog posts—Publish blog posts on related topics in the weeks leading up to the program date.

- Speaking and interviews—Set up speaking and interview gigs for yourself on related topics in the weeks prior to the program.

- Paid ads—If your budget permits, consider purchasing low-cost targeted ads on platforms that your audience frequents, e.g. Facebook or Instagram.

Create a calendar for yourself that defines which marketing and sales activities you plan to employ, how much or how many of each one, and by when you plan to execute each. This will help you see how much effort you need to make, and keep you on track as the date approaches. Remember that each potential participant may need to hear about your program multiple times before they sign up for it, so it's important to stay on schedule with your planned marketing and follow-up activities.

Create promotional tools

Once you've decided which marketing and sales techniques you'll use to promote your program, you're ready to create the promotional tools you'll need.

The minimum tool you'll need for promotion is an online description of the program. As noted above, this could be a page on your own website, or a program listing on an event promotion platform like Eventbrite. Your page should describe the benefits of participating, not simply provide a way to register. Here are suggestions for what your page should include:

- Dates and times of the program
- Where the program will take place (physical location or webinar platform)
- Benefits of participating
- Who is a good candidate to participate
- What will be included in the program
- Who will lead the program, including a brief bio
- Testimonials for the program, or for you as a program leader

- Price
- Link to register

See the *Guide* **Appendix** for a sample public program promo page.

In addition to this, you might also create the additional tools below, as required by the marketing and sales campaign you designed in the previous step.

- Email invitations—You'll want to create a series of these to be sent at intervals throughout the six weeks leading up to your program. Be sure to include benefits of participating in the program. See the *Guide* **Appendix** for an example.
- Verbal pitch—Craft a verbal pitch for your program to use at networking groups or events and in follow-up phone calls.
- Social media post(s)—Create one or more text or video posts promoting your program, to be posted at intervals.
- Event listing(s)—Create listings for any event calendars you plan to use in promotion. Be sure to include benefits of participating, similar to those suggested for a web page.
- Printed flyer/promo card—Design a flyer or promo card to be used for distribution or bulletin boards. See the sample promo pieces in the *Guide* **Appendix** for ideas on what to include.
- Blog post(s)—Write one or more posts on topics related to your program.
- Short talk or talking points—Prepare a related talk or talking points for speaking gigs or interviews.
- Pitch letter—To land speaking gigs or interviews, you'll likely also need an email pitch letter to present yourself as a speaking or interview candidate.
- Paid ad content—If you are purchasing any paid ads, create the text and/or images needed.

Enroll participants

You'll likely be enrolling participants for the entire six weeks leading up to your program date, unless you're lucky enough to sell out your maximum early. You'll typically find yourself continuing your outreach to new program candidates as well as following up repeatedly with people who have heard about your program before.

Don't make the mistake of thinking that attracting new prospective participants is more important than following up with the potential participants you already know about. Experience shows that people who have heard about the program multiple times are more likely to enroll than those who hear about it only once. So don't neglect follow-up in favor of new outreach.

Following up will typically consist of:

- Continuing to send email invitations to the same list of prospective participants
- Continuing to make social media posts about the program
- Continuing to participate in groups or attend networking events where you can announce your program or distribute flyers
- Sending personal emails or texts—or making phone calls—to people you believe are likely candidates

Whenever someone tells you they intend to enroll, make it a practice to immediately register them yourself whenever possible. This will make sure they follow through on their intention, and save you having to pursue them later.

For example, if you're talking with them on the phone, collect their payment info as you speak and enter their enrollment into the program registration page yourself. If you're speaking face to face, ask them to use Venmo or PayPal to send you the registration fee on the spot, and collect their email address to send a welcome email later. If you're texting, messaging, or emailing with someone who declares they wish to enroll, reply immediately with the direct link to register and ask that they do so right away to secure their place.

Don't worry that asking for immediate enrollment makes you seem pushy. What you're actually doing is making their lives easier and giving them better client care. If you think of it like that as you make your request, your participants will view it the same way.

What to do as participants enroll

Send each participant a welcome email. If your registration platform can do so automatically, be sure to set up that feature. Otherwise, send the welcome email as soon as possible after each participant enrolls.

Include the following in your welcome email:

- Your thanks for their registration

- Dates and times for all sessions

- Location and/or access information for the sessions

- A request that they add all session dates and times to their calendar, along with the location and/or access info

- Instructions for what to do if they will miss a session or be late

- Reminder that they need to purchase the book (unless you're providing it), with a purchase link, if possible

- Their pre-work assignment

- Download links for any additional materials you're providing (see the section "Optional participant materials" in *Guide* **Chapter Two**)

- Your refund policy

- How to contact you for questions

See the *Guide* **Appendix** for a sample welcome email for public group programs.

As participants enroll, create a roster of who has registered which includes their name, email, and phone number. You may also choose to include other information you gather about them, such as their location, time zone, or profession.

To make sure your participants remember where and when to attend the first session, I recommend you send them reminders one week, one day, and one hour (for virtual sessions) or two hours (for in-person sessions) before the session begins. Include a reminder to obtain the book and complete the pre-work reading, as well.

What if your program doesn't fill?

If you followed my earlier advice, you set a minimum number of participants you would need for your program to go forward. As your start date approaches, if you haven't yet reached that minimum, you have a decision to make. Should you cancel the program and try again sometime later? Or delay the start date to give yourself more lead time for enrollment? Or even run the underenrolled program anyway to satisfy the folks who already enrolled, build word of mouth, and gain experience as a facilitator?

For help with making your go or no-go decision, and ideas for how to get more participants at the last minute, see "Emergency enrollment measures" in the *Guide* **Appendix**.

Your next steps

Congratulations! You're ready to facilitate your first session. Return to *Guide* **Chapter Two: Facilitating the Program for Groups or Individuals** and pick up with the section "How to facilitate the program." Good luck!

Chapter Four: Marketing and Enrollment for In-House Group Programs

Who should read this chapter

In this chapter, you'll find guidelines for marketing an in-house group program—that is, a program you will offer to an organization like a company, training school, or professional association. If instead, you'll offer a group program that you market to individuals who don't necessarily know each other and who will enroll themselves, you should instead read *Guide* **Chapter Three: Marketing and Enrollment for Public Group Programs**. Or, if you will offer the program as a book discussion group or peer success team, refer instead to *Guide* **Chapter Five: Marketing and Enrollment for Book Groups or Success Teams**.

Choose an audience or target market

Your first necessary step will be to decide what categories of organizations you wish to target. You'll find a description of the most likely individuals to benefit from the program in *Guide* **Chapter One**. Organizations that employ or serve those types of professionals and creatives are the ideal institutions for you to target for in-house programs. Consider organizations like these:

- Companies employing professionals who are expected to build their own book of business, such as accounting firms, law firms, financial management or investment firms, and insurance companies.

- Companies which hire independent contractors who must bring in their own clients, such as real estate agencies or some consulting firms.

- Franchise companies which license independent franchisees to deliver services to the franchisees' own clients.

- Direct sales organizations, also known as multilevel marketing, network marketing, or party plan companies.

- Training schools which prepare individuals in a professional specialty where many must attract their own clients, such as accounting, alternative health, art and design, bodywork, executive or life coaching, financial services, real estate, or therapy.

- Professional associations serving professionals and creatives who must often build their own client base, such as those listed in the *Guide* **Introduction.**

Determine your price range and minimum enrollment

The different types of organizations which could sponsor your in-house programs have differing practices about pricing and payment.

If you'd like to offer your program to a professional association, the usual practice is that the association will enroll interested members, then "split the gate" with you. This doesn't necessarily mean a 50/50 split between you and the association. You could split the proceeds of the program 60/40, 75/25, or 80/20, with the higher percentage going to you.

In this situation, you would agree with the association what price their members will pay to participate, what the split will be between you and the association, and whether there will be any costs deducted from the total the association collects before your portion of the split is calculated.

The best way to approach setting your price and what split will work for you is to first consider the total amount you need to walk away with for this program to be worth your while.

Let's say you'd like to earn at least $2,000 for your in-house program, and you'll have no additional costs to cover. If your program could attract ten participants, that would mean your percentage of the total proceeds would need to equal at least $200 per person ($2,000 ÷ 10). But since the association sponsor will be taking a percentage of the total, the price charged per person will either need to be higher than $200, or the minimum enrollment you'll accept will need to be higher.

For example, if you agree to a 60/40 split of the proceeds, with 60% going to you, the total proceeds would need to be $3,333 ($2,000 ÷ 60%). At a per-participant price of $200, you would need 17 participants ($3,333 ÷ $200). Or, with the same minimum of ten participants as in the example above, the association would need to charge at least $333 per person ($3,333 ÷ 10).

You may need to model several different scenarios to come up with a program price, minimum enrollment, and split of the proceeds that will be acceptable to all. Any time you agree to an in-house program where you will split the gate, it's essential for you to specify a minimum enrollment required for the program to go forward. That's how you can guarantee you will get paid what you require.

When offering your program in-house to a company or training school, they will often prefer to pay you a flat fee rather than split the enrollment proceeds. This is because the sponsor may be paying your full fee themselves, without asking the participants to contribute.

In a flat fee situation, you can still request a higher fee for higher enrollment. For example, you could request a fee of $2,000 for up to eight participants, to be increased by $250 for each additional participant enrolled. You don't need to require a minimum enrollment for a flat fee engagement, as you are requesting to be paid your minimum fee regardless of the number of participants enrolled.

Design a marketing and sales campaign to find sponsors

To successfully land sponsors for your in-house program, you'll need a marketing and sales campaign. While your marketing and sales won't be driven by an upcoming program date (as it would with public programs), you'll still need to plan a campaign to find program sponsors and sell them the program. Here are some of the promotional strategies you should consider:

- Web page—Add a page about your in-house program offering to your existing website.

- Prospect research—Seek out potential sponsors with whom you might have some affinity and obtain their contact information.

- Customized emails and phone calls—Send a series of emails pitching your in-house program to likely targets, and couple them with phone calls. See the *Guide* **Appendix** for a sample email.

- Social media—Make text or video posts periodically about the availability of your program.

- Networking groups and events—Participate in groups and events where you can network with other attendees, seeking out groups and events that will attract potential program sponsors. Consider both in-person and virtual groups and events, which you might find on LinkedIn, Facebook, Meetup, Eventbrite, and many other platforms specific to your locale or audience.

- Personal follow-up—Send personal emails or texts, or make follow-up phone calls, to people you believe are interested in sponsoring your program. You may need to continue doing this even after you've delivered a proposal to the potential sponsor.

- Blog posts—Publish blog posts periodically on related topics.

- Speaking and interviews—Set up speaking and interview gigs for yourself periodically on related topics.

Create a calendar for yourself that integrates marketing and sales activities for your in-house programs with other marketing and sales you plan for your business. This will help you to stay focused on promoting in-house programs while also doing other types of promotion. It's typical to need multiple contacts with a potential sponsor before they commit to setting up an in-house program, so you'll need to keep on top of your planned follow-up activities.

Create marketing tools

Once you've decided which marketing and sales techniques you'll use to market your in-house program, you're ready to create the sales and marketing tools you'll need.

The minimum tool you'll need for marketing is an online description of the program. This will most likely be a page on your own website. Your page should describe the benefits of the program to the sponsor, not only the benefits to participants. See the *Guide* **Appendix** for a sample in-house program promo page.

- Email template—To pitch your program via email, you'll need a template you can customize for each recipient with details about why your program is a good fit for them.

- Verbal pitch—Craft a verbal pitch for your program to use in networking groups or events and in follow-up phone calls.

- Social media posts—Create one or more text or video posts promoting your program offering, to be posted at intervals.

- Blog post(s)—Write one or more posts on topics related to your program.

- Short talk or talking points—Prepare a related talk or talking points for speaking gigs or interviews.

- Pitch letter—To land speaking gigs or interviews, you'll likely also need an email pitch letter to present yourself as a speaking or interview candidate.

Close the sale

It's typical to need multiple contacts with a potential program sponsor before they agree to sponsor an in-house program and set a date. You'll usually find yourself continuing your outreach to new potential sponsors as well as following up repeatedly with people you have contacted before.

Don't make the mistake of thinking that attracting new prospective sponsors is more important than following up with the potential sponsors you already know about. Experience shows that people who have heard about the program multiple times are more likely to hire you than those who hear about it only once. So don't neglect follow-up in favor of new outreach.

Following up will typically consist of:

- Continuing to send customized email pitches, coupled with phone calls, to the same list of prospective sponsors

- Continuing to make social media posts about the program

- Continuing to participate in networking groups or events where you can announce the availability of your program or meet likely sponsors

When your marketing and sales efforts have produced a suitable sponsor with strong interest, you'll need to craft a detailed business proposal that spells out the details of your offering in order to close the sale. See the *Guide* **Appendix** for an example.

Plan to continue following up with the sponsor after you've delivered your proposal. Don't consider the sale closed until you've agreed upon a program date and arranged for payment.

For any type of in-house program, I recommend you ask the sponsor to make a deposit in order to reserve your time. For flat fee sponsors, a non-refundable deposit of 50% is customary. For split-the-gate sponsors, the amount of any deposit is negotiable, and you may also agree to refund the deposit or a portion of it, if the minimum enrollment isn't met.

It's a good practice to ask that the balance owed to you be paid no later than the start date of the program. The method of payment you accept from the program sponsor is up to you, but I recommend you request online payment via PayPal, Stripe, Venmo, or Zelle, rather than waiting for a check to arrive.

Memorialize the terms you and the sponsor have decided on with a letter of agreement which both you and the sponsor sign. I don't recommend skipping this step even when making an arrangement with someone you trust. It's always possible that your key contact person will no longer be with the organization when it's time for your program.

A sample letter of agreement appears in the *Guide* **Appendix**, however, please recognize that if you use this as a model you will be doing so at your own risk. I can't offer you any guarantees that this document will protect your rights under all circumstances and in all jurisdictions.

Provide the program sponsor with tools to enroll participants

Although with in-house programs, you won't be responsible for enrolling the participants, you'll still need to provide the sponsor with tools that make this process easy for them. See the examples in the *Guide* **Appendix** for a public program promo page and a public program email invitation and use these to craft your own samples to share with program sponsors.

What the program sponsor should do as participants enroll

Ask the sponsor to send each participant a welcome email as they enroll, to include the following:

- Thanks for their registration
- Dates and times for all sessions
- Location and/or access information for the sessions
- A request that they add all session dates and times to their calendar, along with the location and/or access details
- Instructions for what to do if they will miss a session or be late
- Reminder that they need to purchase the book (unless you're providing it), with a purchase link, if possible

- Their pre-work assignment
- Download links for any additional materials you're providing (see the section "Optional participant materials" in *Guide* **Chapter Two**)
- The sponsor's refund policy
- Who to contact for questions

See the *Guide* **Appendix** for a sample welcome email for public group programs that you can adapt for in-house programs.

You should also ask the sponsor for a list of participant names, along with their emails and phone numbers, to be delivered no later than a week before the program begins. The sponsor can continue to take registrations for the program up to the start date, so long as they agree to send you information about the new participants right away.

To make sure your participants remember where and when to attend the first session, I recommend you send them reminders one week, one day, and one hour (for virtual sessions) or two hours (for in-person sessions) before the session begins. Include a reminder to obtain the book and complete the pre-work reading, as well.

Don't rely on the program sponsor to send these reminders; it's much better for them to come directly from you.

What if an in-house program doesn't fill?

If you followed my earlier advice, you agreed with the program sponsor on a minimum number of participants needed for your program to go forward. (If you're being paid for the program with a flat fee, a minimum enrollment may not apply, and you can skip to the next section of this chapter.)

As the program start date approaches, if you haven't yet reached minimum enrollment, you and the sponsor will have a decision to make. Should you cancel the program and try again sometime later? Or delay the start date to give the sponsor more lead time for enrollment? Or even run the underenrolled program anyway to satisfy the folks who already enrolled, build word of mouth, and gain experience as a facilitator?

Be sure that whatever decision you and the sponsor make will meet your financial needs. If you don't have confidence the sponsor will be able to increase enrollment, you are fully within your rights to cancel a program for which the minimum hasn't been met. If the sponsor wants to go forward with a smaller number of participants, they should be paying you more per person than you originally agreed. For more help with making a go or no-go decision, and ideas for how the sponsor can get more participants at the last minute, see "Emergency enrollment measures" in the *Guide* **Appendix**.

Your next steps

Congratulations! You're ready to facilitate your first session. Return to *Guide* **Chapter Two: Facilitating the Program for Groups or Individuals** and pick up with the section "How to facilitate the program." Good luck!

Chapter Five: Marketing and Enrollment for Book Groups or Success Teams

Who should read this chapter

In this chapter, you'll find guidelines for marketing a program for a book discussion group or peer success team—that is, a group you will chair or co-chair for a group of peers who wish to support each other at working through the *Overcoming Fear* book together. You will typically not charge a fee to join this group, although you might ask for a small amount of dues simply to cover expenses.

Your success team might be as small as just you and a buddy. If you already have a buddy in mind, you can skip this chapter entirely and return to *Guide* **Chapter Two: Facilitating the Program for Groups or Individuals** and pick up with the section "How to facilitate the program."

If, instead of organizing a peer group, you'll be offering a group program on a paid basis for individuals who will enroll themselves, you should skip this chapter and read *Guide* **Chapter Three: Marketing and Enrollment for Public Group Programs**. Or, if you wish to offer *Overcoming Fear* as an in-house program to an organization, you should read *Guide* **Chapter Four: Marketing and Enrollment for In-House Programs**.

Choose an audience or target market

Your first necessary step will be to decide what audience of individuals you wish to target. You'll find a description of the best candidates for the program in the section "Who are the best candidates to participate" in *Guide* **Chapter One**.

While you can certainly offer your group to anyone who might benefit, you'll have more success when you focus on an audience you already know or have connections to. This is particularly true when you're offering a group like this for the first time.

Consider how much more attractive a group called "Life Coaches: Learn to Overcome the Fear of Self-Promotion Together" would be to those coaches than the more anonymous "Learn to Overcome the Fear of Self-Promotion Together." Or, the attractiveness of "Book Group: Fearless Self-Promotion for Attorneys" or "Designers Book Group: Let's Conquer the Fear of Self-Promotion" to those specific groups.

Yes, you are limiting your reach by pursuing a particular audience, but you are also giving yourself the ability to target that audience more directly. And, once that audience learns of your group, they will be more attracted to it. So, do consider choosing an audience you have a strong affinity with and already have some connections to.

If you belong to a company, training school, or professional association, forming a group from your organization's existing members may be ideal. You may be able to pitch your idea for a group to your company's training or employee activities manager, to your school's department chair, or your professional association's program chair.

Your audience could be local, regional, national, or international, depending on your own existing reach and preferences. If you choose a local audience, you could potentially have your group meet in person. Cafés are popular meeting spots for groups like these to meet. But since the design of the *Overcoming Fear* program requires a series of sessions rather than a one-time meeting, many group leaders prefer to meet online, via video meeting platforms like Zoom, Google Meet, or Whatsapp.

Set your price and minimum enrollment

Most book discussion groups and success teams working through the *Overcoming Fear* book together do not charge a fee to participants. But you may need to charge a small amount of dues in order to cover expenses. For example, you might want to subscribe to a paid Zoom plan in order to hold longer meetings than the 40 minutes Zoom currently allows for free plans. Or, you might use Meetup to attract your group participants and need to pay the subscription fee. Or, you could choose to meet in person at a co-working space which charges a fee to use a private meeting room.

Don't be afraid you will scare away potential participants by charging a small fee. The upside is that folks who pay a fee to be part of a group tend to have better attendance and are more likely to stay engaged than those who participate for free.

Whether or not you choose to charge a fee, decide before you begin to market what minimum number of participants you will need to keep your group active and cover any expenses. While you can successfully operate an *Overcoming Fear* group with only one other participant besides yourself, a suggested minimum number for a group is four. As the start date approaches, you can decide whether you have enough participants to go forward, or if you should delay, cancel, or employ emergency enrollment methods. (See "Emergency enrollment measures" in the *Guide* **Appendix** for more details.)

Set up any registration or payment

Especially if you won't be charging a fee for enrollment, your registration process for a book group or success team may be quite informal. You might ask members to commit by simply sending you an email with their contact info. Any fees could be collected by Venmo, PayPal, or even cash at an in-person meeting.

If you need to reach outside an existing group to recruit members, you may find it helpful to set up a method for participants to enroll themselves and pay any fees. The platform you use could also deliver to your participants a welcome letter with information about how to participate. Options you might consider are:

- A page on an event platform such as Eventbrite or Meetup, which will also allow you to collect fees, if desired.

- A listing on event calendars within Facebook, LinkedIn, or another platform that collects RSVPs. You may need to collect any fees separately if you choose this option.

Design an enrollment campaign

Depending on your audience and whether you have a sponsoring organization, you may need a marketing and sales campaign to successfully fill your program. You should plan to begin promoting your program six weeks before you intend the program to begin.

Activities like those described below will help you create a campaign for your *Overcoming Fear* program. Here are some of the promotional strategies you should consider:

- Web page—Add a page about the program to the website of any sponsoring organization, or create a listing on a platform that accepts event RSVPs, such as Eventbrite, Meetup, Facebook, or LinkedIn.

- Broadcast email—Send a series of emails to your sponsoring organization's mailing list, or assemble a new mailing list from your own contacts.

- Social media—Make text or video posts about the program periodically leading up to the program date, and ask any sponsoring organization to do the same.

- Event listings—Create listings for the program on event calendars in addition to the platform where you're taking registrations. Consider general calendars like Facebook or LinkedIn, as well as others specific to your target audience or geographic area.

- Flyer/promo card distribution—Make flyers or promo cards available at events you're attending, and venues that attract your target audience.

- Networking groups and events—Participate in groups and events where you can network with other attendees, seeking out groups and events that will attract potential participants. Consider both in-person and virtual groups and events, which you might find on LinkedIn, Facebook, Meetup, Eventbrite, and many other platforms specific to your locale or audience.

- Personal follow-up—Send personal emails or texts, or make follow-up phone calls, to people you believe are interested in the program.

Create a calendar for yourself that defines which marketing and sales activities you plan to employ, how much or how many of each one, and by when you plan to execute each. This will help you see how much effort you need to make, and keep you on track as the date approaches. Remember that each potential participant may need to hear about your program multiple times before they sign up for it, so it's important to stay on schedule with your planned marketing and follow-up activities.

Create promotional tools

Once you've decided which marketing and sales techniques you'll use to promote your program, you're ready to create the promotional tools you'll need.

Especially if you need to reach outside an existing group to recruit members, you may need an online description of the program for promotion. As noted above, this could be a page on any sponsoring organization's website, or an event listing on a platform such as Eventbrite, Meetup, Facebook, or LinkedIn. Or, if your primary method of promotion will be sending emails, you may be able to rely on an email description alone, and not need an online description.

Your page, listing, or email should describe the benefits of participating, not simply provide a way to register. Here are suggestions for what your promo piece should include:

- Dates and times of the program
- Where the program will take place (physical location or webinar platform)
- Benefits of participating
- Who is a good candidate to participate
- What will be included in the program
- Who will lead the program, including a brief bio of the leader or statement that members will take turn leading
- Price, if any
- Instructions to register

See the *Guide* **Appendix** for a sample book group/success team promo page or email copy.

In addition to this, you might also create the additional tools below, as required by the marketing and sales campaign you designed in the previous step.

- Email invitations—You'll want to create a series of these to be sent at intervals throughout the six weeks leading up to your program. Be sure to include benefits of participating in the program. See the *Guide* **Appendix** for an example.
- Verbal pitch—Craft a verbal pitch for your program to use in networking groups or events and in follow-up phone calls.
- Social media post(s)—Write one or more posts promoting your program, to be posted at intervals.
- Event listing(s)—Create listings for any event calendars you plan to use in promotion. Be sure to include benefits of participating, similar to those suggested for a web page.

- Printed flyer/promo card—Design a flyer or promo card to be used for distribution or bulletin boards. See the sample promo pieces in the *Guide* **Appendix** for ideas on what to include.

Enroll participants

You may be enrolling participants for the entire six weeks leading up to your program date, unless you're lucky enough to enroll your maximum early. You'll typically find yourself continuing your outreach to new program candidates as well as following up repeatedly with people who have heard about your program before.

Don't make the mistake of thinking that attracting new prospective participants is more important than following up with the potential participants you already know about. Experience shows that people who have heard about the program multiple times are more likely to enroll than those who hear about it only once. So don't neglect follow-up in favor of new outreach.

Following up will typically consist of:

- Continuing to send email invitations to the same list of prospective participants
- Continuing to make social media posts about the program
- Continuing to participate in groups or attend networking events where you can announce your program or distribute flyers
- Sending personal emails or texts—or making phone calls—to people you believe are likely candidates

Whenever someone tells you they intend to enroll, make it a practice to immediately register them yourself whenever possible. This will make sure they follow through on their intention, and save you having to pursue them later.

For example, if you're talking with them on the phone, collect any payment info as you speak and enter their enrollment into any program registration page yourself. If you're speaking face to face, ask them to use Venmo or PayPal to send you any registration fee on the spot, and collect their email address to send a welcome email later. If you're texting, messaging, or emailing with someone who declares they wish to enroll, reply immediately with the details to register and ask that they do so right away to secure their place.

Don't worry that asking for immediate enrollment makes you seem pushy. What you're actually doing is making their lives easier and giving them better member care. If you think of it like that as you make your request, your participants will view it the same way.

What to do as participants enroll

Send each participant a welcome email. If your registration platform can do so automatically, be sure to set up that feature. Otherwise, send the welcome email as soon as possible after each participant enrolls.

Include the following in your welcome email:

- Your thanks for their registration
- Dates and times for all sessions if this has already been determined, or if not, proposed meeting times with a request to vote for their preference
- Location and/or access information for the sessions
- A request that they add all session dates and times to their calendar, along with the location and/or access details
- Instructions for what to do if they will miss a session or be late
- Reminder that they need to purchase the book, with a purchase link, if possible
- Their pre-work assignment
- Download links for any additional materials you're providing (see the section "Optional participant materials" in *Guide* **Chapter Two**)

- Your refund policy, if any

- How to contact you for questions

See the *Guide* **Appendix** for a sample welcome email for public group programs, which you can adapt for a peer group.

As participants enroll, create a roster of who has registered which includes their name, email, and phone number. You may also choose to include other information you gather about them, such as their location, time zone, or profession.

To make sure your participants remember where and when to attend the first session, I recommend you send them reminders one week, one day, and one hour (for virtual sessions) or two hours (for in-person sessions) before the session begins.

What if your program doesn't fill?

If you followed my earlier advice, you set a minimum number of participants you would need for your program to go forward. As your start date approaches, if you haven't yet reached that minimum, you have a decision to make. Should you cancel the program and try again sometime later? Or delay the start date to give yourself more lead time for enrollment? Or even run the underenrolled program anyway to satisfy the folks who already enrolled?

For help with making your go or no-go decision, and ideas for how to get more participants at the last minute, see "Emergency enrollment measures" in the *Guide* **Appendix**.

Your next steps

Congratulations! You're ready to facilitate your first session. Return to *Guide* **Chapter Two: Facilitating the Program for Groups or Individuals**, and pick up with the section "How to facilitate the program." Good luck!

Chapter Six: Coaching Individuals

Who should read this chapter

The *Overcoming Fear* program can be easily adapted for use as a one-on-one coaching program which you offer to existing coaching clients or new prospective clients. If you're interested in offering *Overcoming Fear* as a one-on-one program rather than solely to groups, you should read this chapter instead of, or in addition to, *Guide* **Chapters Three through Five**.

Choose an audience or target market

To offer *Overcoming Fear* to your current clients, you'll need to decide which of your clients would benefit, list talking points to bring up in a future coaching session, and agree with each client how to best integrate *Overcoming Fear* with their regular coaching.

Talking points you might bring up with a current client include:

- Describing what you've noticed about their struggles with fear, resistance, or the inner critic

- Asking what they believe is holding them back from promoting themselves more successfully

- Challenging them to take on the obstacles that are preventing them from being more effective at marketing and sales

To offer *Overcoming Fear* as a package to prospective coaching clients, you'll need to choose an audience, set your price, create promotional tools, include this option in your existing marketing campaigns for coaching, and enroll participants.

As with other formats for the program, you'll find a description of likely candidates in the section "Who are the best candidates to participate" in *Guide* **Chapter One**. It will best serve your coaching practice if the audience you choose for *Overcoming Fear* is either the same audience you market your regular coaching services to, or a subset of that audience. That way, all of your marketing and sales efforts will be able to work together.

While you can certainly offer the program to anyone who might benefit, you'll have more success when you focus on an audience you already know or have connections to. This is particularly true when you're new to coaching or offering a coaching program like this for the first time.

Consider how much more attractive an offer headlined "Life Coaches: Learn to Overcome the Fear of Self-Promotion" would be to those coaches than the more anonymous "Learn to Overcome the Fear of Self-Promotion." Or, the attractiveness of "Coaching Program: Fearless Self-Promotion for Attorneys" or "Coaching Program for Designers: Conquer the Fear of Self-Promotion" to those specific groups.

Yes, you are limiting your reach by pursuing a particular audience, but you are also giving yourself the ability to target that audience more directly. And, once that audience learns of your offer, they will be more attracted to it. So, do consider choosing an audience you have a strong affinity with and already have some connections to.

Your audience could be local, regional, national, or international, depending on your own existing reach and preferences. If you choose a local audience, you could potentially have your clients meet you in person. But as with regular coaching relationships, many coaches prefer to meet online, via video meeting platforms like Zoom, Google Meet, or Whatsapp.

Establish your price and working arrangement

During a regular coaching engagement, you might integrate *Overcoming Fear* by:

- Putting coaching on hold for five weeks while you coach them through the program with a session each week

- Dedicating a portion of each regular coaching session (weekly or biweekly) to the program for a period of five to ten weeks
- Alternating regular weekly coaching sessions with weekly *Overcoming Fear* sessions for ten to eighteen weeks
- Any other arrangement that would serve both you and the client

You might continue to charge the same fee you would charge the client for regular coaching that has a similar time commitment, which is how I've charged for *Overcoming Fear* as a one-on-one program in the past. Or, you could charge a higher fee for the period of time you're using the program with an existing client.

For a new client to whom you're offering *Overcoming Fear* as a standalone coaching program, you might package the program as:

- Nine weekly sessions of 45-60 minutes per session
- Five biweekly or monthly sessions of 60-90 minutes per session
- Any other arrangement that would serve both you and the client

A common practice when offering a coaching program of fixed length would be to quote a fixed price for the full program, which you might collect all at once at the beginning, or in installments over the length of the program. When coaching individuals, you won't be able to leverage your time as you can when coaching/facilitating groups. So, you'll need to charge more than you would when offering *Overcoming Fear* as a group program. Make sure the price you charge is adequate to compensate you for the required time.

Create promotional tools

To offer *Overcoming Fear* to your existing clients as a one-on-one program, you may decide not to create any promotional tools at all. But to offer *Overcoming Fear* as a standalone coaching program for potential clients, you'll typically need an online description of the program on your website. If you don't yet have a site, you could also include the same information in a PDF, brochure, or flyer.

Your promo page or promo piece should describe the benefits of participating, not simply provide a way to enroll. Here are suggestions for what your promo should include:

- Where the program will take place (physical location or webinar platform)
- Benefits of participating
- Who is a good candidate to participate
- What will be included in the program
- Who will lead/coach the program, including a brief bio
- Testimonials for the program, or for you as a program leader/coach
- Price
- How and where to enroll

See the *Guide* **Appendix** for a sample individual coaching program promo page.

Include the program in your existing marketing and sales campaigns for coaching

In addition to the promo page or piece described above, you might also create the additional tools below, as appropriate for the marketing and sales campaigns you are already conducting—or plan to conduct—for one-on-one coaching.

- Email promos—You'll want to include a mention of the *Overcoming Fear* program in any emails you send promoting your coaching services. As with the promo page/piece described above, be sure to include benefits of participating in the program.

- Verbal pitch—Craft a verbal pitch for the program to use in networking groups or events and in follow-up phone calls.

- Social media post(s)—Create one or more text or video posts promoting the program, to be posted at intervals.

- Printed flyer/promo card—Design a flyer or promo card to be used for distribution or bulletin boards. See the sample promo pieces in the *Guide* **Appendix** for ideas on what to include.

- Blog post(s)—Write one or more posts on topics related to the program.

- Short talk or talking points—Prepare a related talk or talking points for speaking gigs or interviews.

- Paid ad content—If you are purchasing any paid ads, create the text and/or images needed.

Enroll participants

When offering *Overcoming Fear* as a one-on-one coaching program, you'll typically be integrating your follow-up and enrollment with the activities you're already doing—or planning— to enroll clients in your regular coaching services. This usually involves continuing your outreach to new candidates as well as following up repeatedly with people who have heard about your offers before.

Don't make the mistake of thinking that attracting new prospective participants is more important than following up with the potential participants you already know about. Experience shows that people who have heard about your offers multiple times are more likely to enroll than those who hear about them only once. So don't neglect follow-up in favor of new outreach.

Following up will typically consist of:

- Continuing to send email promos to the same list of prospective participants

- Continuing to make social media posts about the program

- Continuing to participate in groups or attend networking events where you can announce your program or distribute flyers
- Sending personal emails or texts—or making phone calls—to people you believe are likely candidates

Whenever someone tells you they intend to enroll, make it a practice to immediately confirm them whenever possible. This will make sure they follow through on their intention, and save you having to pursue them later.

For example, if you're talking with them on the phone, collect their payment info as you speak and schedule their coaching sessions. If you're speaking face to face, ask them to use Venmo or PayPal to send you the enrollment fee on the spot, schedule at least their first session, and collect their email address to send a welcome email later. If you're texting, messaging, or emailing with someone who declares they wish to enroll, reply immediately with the details to pay and schedule, asking that they do so right away to secure their spot on your calendar.

Don't worry that asking for immediate enrollment makes you seem pushy. What you're actually doing is making their lives easier and giving them better client care. If you think of it like that as you make your request, your participants will view it the same way.

What to do as participants enroll

Send each participant—whether they are existing clients or new clients—a welcome or confirmation email. If you're using a payment platform that can send a welcome message automatically, be sure to set up that feature. Otherwise, send a welcome email as soon as possible after each participant enrolls.

If your participant is an existing coaching client, send them a confirmation email that includes the following:

- Your thanks for their enrollment

- How the *Overcoming Fear* program will be integrated with their regular coaching

- Schedule for their program sessions, or how to schedule them

- Reminder that they need to purchase the book (unless you're providing it), with a purchase link, if possible

- Their pre-work assignment

- Download links for any additional materials you're providing (see the section "Optional participant materials" in *Guide* **Chapter Two**)

If your participant is a new client enrolling in the program only, send them a welcome email that includes the following:

- Your thanks for their enrollment

- How to schedule their program sessions

- Location and/or access information for the sessions

- A request that they add all session dates and times to their calendar, along with the location and/or access details

- Instructions for what to do if they will miss a session or be late

- Reminder that they need to purchase the book (unless you're providing it), with a purchase link, if possible

- Their pre-work assignment

- Download links for any additional materials you're providing (see the section "Optional participant materials" in *Guide* **Chapter Two**)

- Your refund policy

- How to contact you for questions

See the *Guide* **Appendix** for a sample welcome email for public group programs, which you can adapt for individual clients.

To make sure your participant remembers where and when to attend the first session, I recommend you send them a reminder one day before the session begins. Include a reminder to obtain the book and complete the pre-work reading, as well.

Your next steps

Congratulations! You're ready to coach your first session. Return to *Guide* **Chapter Two: Facilitating the Program for Groups or Individuals** and pick up with the section "How to facilitate the program." Good luck!

Chapter Seven: Tips and Tricks for Leaders

Skills and guidelines you'll need

When you begin facilitating *Overcoming Fear* for the first time, you may be a coach who is new to facilitating, a trainer/facilitator who is new to coaching, or you may have many years of experience with coaching and facilitating both. Regardless, I suggest you read through this chapter for how the skills you already know can best be adapted to leading *Overcoming Fear*.

If you've never tried group coaching before, you'll find that coaching a group of people at once is different from both teaching a class and from one-on-one coaching. You need to have even more awareness of all that's happening than you do when coaching an individual. You must be aware of each participant, of the group as a whole, and of the timeline and structure for your session. When you're doing this online, it can sometimes feel like being the host of a call-in radio show with no producer to screen incoming calls, and no commercial break giving you a chance to regain your composure.

Keep in mind that your primary job when leading an *Overcoming Fear* program is to help participants develop their own abilities, not to act as an information-based teacher or consultant. Even when you know a great deal about effective self-promotion, you'll want to avoid supplying answers to "how-to" questions about sales and marketing during your sessions. Use the tips below to lead your sessions in a more productive direction when how-to questions arise. And if you do have the appropriate expertise, by all means suggest participants book a private session with you, view your videos, read your book, etc.

Below you'll first find guidelines for using facilitation skills, then suggestions for how to use coaching skills, and finally, tips for managing specific situations that may arise in leading *Overcoming Fear* programs. When you integrate facilitation skills with coaching skills and add in techniques specific to the *Overcoming Fear* program, you'll become a powerful and effective leader.

Essential facilitation skills

- Manage time—To get everything done in each session, you'll need to keep tight control of the timeline. Since the main content of the program is written out in the *Overcoming Fear* book, your best practice is to rely on participants to read the assigned chapter(s) before coming to class. Then there's no need to spend much time lecturing; you can allow the most time for exercises and questions.

- Listen at multiple levels—In addition to listening to what each participant is saying out loud, also listen to what's going on with them beneath their words. And, pay attention to what's happening with the group as a whole. Allow what you hear and sense to guide your responses and how you direct the flow of the sessions.

- Maintain a fair balance between teaching, coaching, and group interaction—You'll have certain points to teach in each session, but there will also be many appropriate moments for coaching. Spending a few minutes to coach just one person is fine, as others listening will learn from this also. Incorporating some group interaction, such as brainstorming or a round of debriefing, should also be part of every session.

- Keep participants engaged—Ask video participants to leave their cameras on and request that in-person participants put their phones away. Plan to change modalities often, switching between lecture, exercises, and group interaction frequently.

- Get yourself out of the way—Strive to be "the guide on the side, not the sage on the stage" when leading your sessions. Allow the personal experiences and realizations of the participants to drive the learning, rather than relying solely on your wisdom as a teacher.

- Insist on the bottom line—Giving each participant a chance to report their experience is essential for the program to do its magic. But if you allow everyone to tell a story along with their report, there will be no time for anything else. Keep the session moving by asking participants to "bottom-line" their narrative.

- Get some people to talk more—Invite everyone to participate by calling on participants who don't speak up on their own. Ask participants specific, open-ended questions. Rather than, "Did you do the homework?" ask, "How did the homework go for you?" If you sense a participant is hesitant to make a mistake, remind them there are no wrong answers in this program.

- Get some people to talk less—If you have a participant who tends to dominate the conversation, interject with: "Let's hear from someone else." If necessary, speak to overly talkative participants outside class and ask them to notice when they're talking more than others.

- Encourage brainstorming—When you invite participants to contribute ideas, let them know all suggestions are welcome. Model the use of "Yes, and…" responses to encourage more ideas rather than rejecting any of those suggested. If someone is clearly on the wrong track, steer them gently elsewhere with "Yes, and you might also try…"

- Be flexible—What happens in sessions can be unpredictable. Even though you have a timeline to follow, you may need to adjust it on the fly if a juicy opportunity for learning appears, or a participant is struggling, or an interruption takes up time. Allow yourself to dance with whatever occurs and adapt it to best serve your participants.

Coaching skills to increase learning

- Design the alliance—Working with the *Overcoming Fear* program requires participants to expand their comfort zone, show vulnerability, and be honest about their inner thoughts, so you'll want to create an atmosphere of safety. In your first session, it's helpful to incorporate elements that will encourage full participation. For example, request compliance with a confidentiality agreement, get permission to coach them on obstacles, let them know you'll call on them if they don't speak, or ask them what kind of feedback they'd like from you.

- Ask powerful questions—In addition to the questions participants will be guided to ask themselves when reading the *Overcoming Fear* book, be prepared to ask participants to look more deeply at their beliefs and behavior with questions like: "Why is this important to you?" "How will you know when you've made progress?" "What would you change next time?" "How committed are you to making this different?" "What strengths can you leverage to address this?" or "What insights are you taking away today?"

- Answer a question with a question—The classic coach's answer to a "how-to" question is: "I don't know; what do you think?" Nine times out of ten, the participant will then proceed to answer their own question. If the participant replies, "I'm not sure," try asking, "Well, if you did know, what would it be?" You'll be surprised how often this works.

- Help them learn to fish—Another approach to answering "how-to" questions is responding with: "How would you find that out?" Even complex questions can usually be answered by a book, blog, video, podcast, website, workshop, or consulting with a professional. You may wish to familiarize yourself with resources to provide additional help to your participants, and get to know the work of relevant experts you might refer to.

- Articulate what's going on—Listening to a participant's words and summarizing for them what you notice makes them feel heard. When you hear something that isn't being fully recognized, state what you're noticing so participants can become aware of it also. At times, you may need to reframe what you hear to give it a deeper impact. For example, if a participant says, "I don't think I can do this because I'm afraid of being rejected," you could respond with, "You've just achieved a goal of this program—you've identified your primary fear as rejection."

- Invoke intuition—Allow the intuitive voice of both your participants and yourself to be expressed. Notice what you're sensing or feeling is going on with a participant or the group as a whole. Ask participants questions that call on their intuition like replying to "I don't know" with "What part of you might know?" or "What would your future self say?"

- Balance problem-solving with learning—Your participants may want to focus on resolving their specific problems. But the *Overcoming Fear* program also lends itself to a significant amount of valuable learning about issues like self-sabotaging behavior, inner critic monologues, and beliefs about money and success. When time permits, don't jump straight to solving the problem at hand. Take some time to explore what is happening and how your participant feels about it. Then ask them to sum up what they have learned before moving on to looking for a solution.

Coaching skills to encourage action

- Forward the action—*Overcoming Fear* is an action-oriented program, so it's crucial for you as the facilitator to keep participants moving forward. While you may spend time during a session exploring a participant's learning, be sure to lead them to an action step before the session ends. Ask questions like, "What's your next step?" and "How could you make that different?"

- Hold them accountable—The responsibility for taking action always rests with the participant. When you make requests of participants or give them assignments, ask them to agree. When a participant expresses a desire to take a certain step, ask for a commitment. "When will you do that?" is a simple phrase you can use in either case. You can also spend time at the beginning of each session asking participants to report back on what they've accomplished.

- Tell them to quit—When you hear participants struggling with lagging motivation or fear that has them frozen, try challenging them to give up: "Getting more business seems like it's hard for you. Do you want to quit?" Most participants will respond testily with something like, "Quit? What do you mean, quit?" Once you've gotten a rise out of them, a good direction to go next is to ask for a higher level of commitment: "On a scale of 1 to 10, how committed are you to getting more business?" then, "Okay, what are you willing to do about it?"

- Acknowledge what's working—Your participants may come to sessions with a list of failures and problems to be worked on. To help keep them motivated, notice and remind them about what they're doing right. Help them learn to reward themselves for improvement rather than insisting on perfection. Yours may be the only voice they hear to counter their inner critic, so make sure part of your message in every session is positive.

- Challenge past the comfort zone—Your participants may need an extra push from you to move into scary territory. This may be particularly true when you're working with clients one-on-one, without the enthusiasm of a group buoying them up. Notice when participants are holding themselves back, and request that they try on a new way of being. One technique is fake-it-till-you-make-it, also known as act-as-if. Suggest that they act as if they were fearless, just while practicing the new skills they're learning.

- Invite woo-woo practices—You may already use techniques in your coaching or your personal life that have more to do with healing or spirituality than business. If so, don't be afraid to take your participants into woo-woo territory. Pay attention to their ideas about how to practice what you're teaching them. Participants may already be writing in a journal, using visualizations, or meditating. Ask more about these activities, and you may find that approaches such as hypnotherapy, energy work, or prayer are also welcome resources.

Coaching skills to incorporate group energy

- Call on group wisdom—When a participant asks a "how-to" question, try throwing it out to the group instead of responding yourself. You might call on a group member who you believe has personal experience with the subject, or simply say, "Who has a response to that?" This models resourcefulness for your participants and helps to develop their self-reliance.

- Let participants coach each other—After your participants have a chance to see how you work with them individually, give them some space to coach each other. This will increase the atmosphere of support and commitment. Some groups will begin doing this spontaneously; in others, you may need to ask, "What might I say to Janey right now?" in order to get them started.

- Coach the winners—In every group, there will be some participants who leap ahead of the others. Don't fall into the trap of thinking they are doing fine so they don't need much "air time," or that you should focus your attention on those who need more help. The winners are the people who are most likely to become champions for your program, and they deserve your very best coaching. If you give them space to shine, they will inspire the others in the group.

- Support the stragglers—You may also have a participant or two who just can't seem to move forward, due to difficult circumstances or self-sabotage. Don't let them drag down the whole group. If needed, encourage these participants to lower their sights to more realistic improvement goals. Then acknowledge them for each small bit of progress they make.

Techniques specific to *Overcoming Fear: Book* Chapter One

- Raising awareness of fear—Participants may say they can't always tell when they're afraid, or they notice sabotaging emotions that aren't actually fear. Remind them that the word "fear" is used in this program to represent a range of emotions and behaviors, such as resistance, procrastination, and the inner critic. Ask them to notice any time they avoid following through on their self-promotion intentions, or seem to be sabotaging promotional activities, and to label what they're feeling then as "fear" for purposes of this program.

- Acceptance of fear—You may encounter participants who refuse to accept their fear or object to doing that. Encourage them to let go of any self-judgment about their feelings. Ask them not to think of these emotions as wrong or bad, but simply present. Tell them that accepting their negative feelings exist is essential for beginning to dissolve them. Request that they try to allow them—for now—just for the length of the program.

- Moving ahead despite fear—A participant may find themselves blocked by self-sabotaging beliefs or behaviors, and not able to move forward easily. Suggest that they try taking very small steps at first, and gradually move toward more difficult actions. You might also point them to **Book Chapter Seven: Quick Fixes for Fearful Moments** for ideas on how to move forward while continuing to work on overcoming their fear.

Techniques specific to *Overcoming Fear: Book* Chapter Two

- Leaning on strengths—Some participants may have difficulty identifying strengths they might lean on when self-promoting. Ask them what they identify as a weakness that they believe gets in their way, and reframe that as a strength. For example, introversion can be a strength because introverts are often good at in-depth, one-on-one conversations. Ask the participant themselves, or the larger group, to suggest ways in which a particular weakness might be used as a strength.

- Holding the Practice Loop as a cycle—Sometimes participants want the Practice Loop to produce immediate results, allowing them to quickly eliminate obstacles simply because they practiced. Remind them it's called a loop because it needs to be repeated. Each cycle through the loop will create gradual improvement which will build over time.

- Diagnosing hidden fears—A participant may claim that their real obstacle is procrastination, disorganization, busy-ness, etc., rather than any form of fear. Coach them to discover the root cause of the problem they name by asking repeatedly, "What's causing that?" "Why can't you do it?" or "Why aren't you doing it?" Most participants will eventually name a form of fear, resistance, or the inner critic hiding underneath the obstacle they named. If they don't, ask them to use the last cause they identified as their "fear" for the purpose of this program.

Techniques specific to *Overcoming Fear: Book* Chapter Three

- Identifying the voice of the inner critic—If participants have trouble distinguishing inner critic dialogue from true inner guidance, such as their intuition or gut feelings, provide them with the following clues. The inner critic typically uses insulting language, and says the same things repeatedly. The voice will often feel like it's mean or nagging. It frequently uses the same words that were used to criticize you by a parent/teacher figure in your past. If the voice feels like it's out of your control, or an attack from outside, it's almost certainly the inner critic talking.

- Practicing inner critic disputation—Learning to dispute the inner critic can take practice, so you may need to reassure participants that this is a skill they can learn over time. Remind them there are three different approaches to dispute the inner critic: present evidence to the contrary, give an alternative explanation, or question the usefulness of the thought. Point out the disputation examples in **Book Chapter Three**. If participants need more help with disputation, suggest they search online for "dispute inner critic examples."

Techniques specific to *Overcoming Fear*: **Book Chapter Four**

- Identifying fears—Some participants may find it difficult to identify which of the seven fears they're experiencing, or believe none of them fit. Remind them of the different approaches to identify their fear which are described **in Book Chapter Four**. If they're still not sure, ask them to describe an instance of self-promotion fear, and see if you or the group can name the fear for them. You can also give them permission to coin their own name for their fear. So long as they can identify a specific fear to work with, it doesn't matter so much what they call it.

- Choosing one primary fear—If a participant can't name which of their fears is the most common or troublesome, suggest they choose the fear that interferes the most with having conversations with people, rather than any other form of self-promotion. Remind them that choosing a specific fear to work on can be just for the length of this program. They can always choose another fear to work on later.

Techniques specific to *Overcoming Fear: Book* Chapter Five

- Resistance to making friends with fear—Some participants may resist the idea of making friends with their fear. They may view their fear as an enemy, or be ashamed of it. Remind them of the program's ground rule to maintain compassionate awareness about their emotions, beliefs, and performance. Ask them to suspend critical judgment for a time, and try out the making-friends approach as an experiment.

- Selecting the best antidote—Participants may not be able to choose which antidote seems right to counteract their fear. The book's suggested antidote for their chosen fear may not seem like a good fit, or perhaps their identified fear has a unique name not in the book. If another of the book's antidotes seems better, they can select a different one. You can also ask the group to brainstorm on possible antidotes for the participant's named fear, or grant them permission to design their own antidote.

Techniques specific to *Overcoming Fear: Book* Chapter Six

- How to develop an antidote—A participant may not be able to come up with a strategy they believe will work to build up their fear antidote. First, make sure they're clear about what antidote they're trying to develop. Then, verify they've read all the antidote-building options in **Book** **Chapter Six**. If they're still unclear, ask the group to brainstorm possible strategies for them, or suggest some yourself. Ask them to choose one strategy to try at least for now. They can always pick another one later.

Techniques specific to *Overcoming Fear: Book* Chapter Seven

- Finding quick fixes that work—If a participant can't identify a quick fix that seems right for them, first make sure they've already tried some of the fixes they don't believe will work. For a participant who is still stuck on this point, ask the group to brainstorm possible fixes for them, suggest some yourself, or coach them to discover new possibilities. Ask them to try some of the new ideas before discarding them in advance.

Techniques specific to *Overcoming Fear: Book* Chapter Eight

- Resistance to building relationships—Some participants may object to the idea that building relationships will help with the issues they're experiencing. Rather than trying to persuade them of this, ask them to suspend their disbelief long enough to try the skills practice suggested in **Book Chapter Eight**. Then gently allow their personal experience with relationship-building, and the reports on this they hear from other participants, to begin dissolving their resistance.

- Obstacles to building relationships—Participants may name obstacles that block them from building more relationships, such as introversion or shyness, neurodiversity, lacking a personal network, living in a remote area, disliking social media, and more. Reassure them that it's possible for anyone to build more relationships by seeking out congenial, like-minded people. Challenge them to identify approaches that will surpass the limitations they believe are holding them back, and assist them with coaching, group brainstorming, or easy-to-try suggestions.

Troubleshooting logistical and business issues

In addition to facilitation and coaching challenges, you may also encounter logistical problems and business-related difficulties when leading the program. Some of the most common issues and my suggested solutions appear below.

- Participant misses a session — Address this at the kickoff meeting by asking them to contact you in advance if they know they will be absent, or after the fact if they missed the session unexpectedly. Invite them to send you an email report that you can forward to the group, which will help keep them motivated. Provide them with a recording of the missed session and request that they review it to catch up. If it seems necessary, offer to schedule a 15-minute live catch-up session with them.

- Participant arrives late to a session — If time permits, have them report some of their experience from the past week, even if that segment of the session is over. If there's no time for this, ask them to email a report to you later on, so they'll still get a chance to check in.

- Participant wants to drop out — Try to coach them about this decision first, in case they are letting their fear run the show. If their rationale for dropping out withstands coaching, then let them go graciously with your best wishes. It won't serve you to insist they stay, as a reluctant player can damage the whole team.

- Paid participant wants their money back — If you made a guarantee of satisfaction, issue a refund promptly. If you didn't, you may have no obligation to refund their money (but you may wish to do so anyway to maintain their goodwill). It's good practice to include a refund clause on your enrollment page or in your welcome letter to make your policy clear. (See the *Guide* **Appendix** for a sample welcome email with a refund policy.) You may want to suggest prorating the refund according to how far along they are in the program, or offer to transfer the participant to a future program.

- Participant is disruptive, uncooperative, or overly negative— Ask them to leave the program, even if you have to refund their money. Keep the good participants happy by ensuring them a positive experience in a safe space.

- Group isn't working well together—Personality clashes do happen. And sometimes participants will enter a group with some negative personal history between them. If the clash can't be easily resolved, consider splitting the group into two sections, or take one person out of the group and coach them individually. You may lose some of your time, but gain plenty of gratitude from the remaining group members.

- Session recording fails—When one or more participants miss a session and you don't have the promised recording to share with them, fill in the gap with a make-up session or recording. You can offer a live make-up session for just those who missed the earlier one, or make a recording for them on your own.

- Tech platform or meeting location not available—If you can't hold a session due to technical or logistical difficulties, try to reschedule it as soon as possible. You may have to move a live session to video, or deliver the lost session twice at different make-up times to accommodate everyone in the group being able to attend.

Your next steps

While the suggestions above will help you be an effective facilitator, your own continued experience in leading the program will help even more. After each session, take a few moments to note anything that went particularly well that you'd like to repeat in a future session. Also, note any rough spots, where you feel you could have done better, or you weren't sure what to do in the moment. Consider how you could have made those situations flow more smoothly, and keep track of your ideas for improvement.

Before leading your next session, look over your past notes as well as reviewing my suggestions in this chapter. Over time, you'll internalize both my guidance and your own to become an outstanding facilitator.

Chapter Eight: How to Keep the Work Alive

Continuing the *Overcoming Fear* work

Once your program ends, you and your participants may choose to continue working with the *Overcoming Fear* material, either separately or together.

Described below are suggestions to help participants keep the work alive for themselves, or keep the group going with you as facilitator, or enroll participants in your coaching or training services. You can choose whichever options would best serve your participants and your own vision for how the *Overcoming Fear* program fits into your business, career, or community service goals.

Help participants keep the work going

In the final session of the program, make sure each participant has drafted their own fear management plan, as described in **Guide Chapter Two**. Ask them to make a commitment to continue working with their plan.

To lock in their commitment to continue the work, you might encourage each participant to set progress goals for themselves. For example, ask them to award themselves a letter grade on some aspect of self-promotion as of today, then calendar a date to check in with themselves on how they've improved. This could sound like: "Today, I'd give myself a 'C' on managing my fear of rejection. In two months, I'd like to deserve a 'B'."

You could also suggest that participants form a practice pod to continue working together without you. If you provide them with each other's contact information, they can organize this themselves.

Ways to continue a group

Sometimes participants in a group program will themselves suggest that their group continue working with you after the program ends. It has happened to me many times that either an entire group or a subset of it wants to keep going past the planned end date. Of course, you can make this suggestion yourself as well.

You might propose to repeat the entire program from beginning to end, as the second time through, participants would take all their learning to a deeper level. Or, you could drop the sessions covering the first three chapters of the book and begin again with identifying their fear in *Book* **Chapter Four**. With that approach, participants might choose to focus on a different self-promotion fear to work with this time.

Another approach would be to set up a biweekly or monthly check-in session with the group that you facilitate. Each participant would have a chance to report on their progress with working their fear management plan. Then you could provide coaching, ask another participant to act as coach, or facilitate group brainstorming on issues presented by one participant or several in the group. At the end of the session, you would ask each participant their next steps.

For either of the options above, if your participants originally paid a fee for your group, they will also expect to pay a fee to continue in a new format. I have had paid groups continue on for months, and even years, after they first began, because I offered them options like these.

An unpaid option to keep your participants in touch with each other, and with you, is to hold a group reunion periodically. You can schedule a date and time for the group to gather online or in person and check in with each other. A meeting like this once per quarter or twice per year will keep the work alive and continue your business relationship with these participants. I've used this reunion strategy many times with groups that worked well together and supported each other's success.

Enrolling participants in ongoing coaching or other learning programs

Whether your program is conducted with one individual or a group, most of your participants will be likely candidates for other services you offer. Don't make the mistake of assuming they will let you know about their interest without an invitation from you.

At the end of your final session, offer to schedule a no-cost follow-up meeting with each participant if they take the time to fill out an evaluation form. At that meeting, they'll have one more chance to ask you their personal questions about the work they've just completed in your program. On your evaluation form, you can ask for helpful feedback, testimonial quotes, and what interest they have in your other offerings. Then schedule a one-on-one conversation with each person to discuss their next steps, and if appropriate, enroll them in further coaching or another program with you.

Whether or not a participant chooses to continue working with you immediately after their program ends, ask their permission to add them to your mailing list and social media connections. In addition, add them to your own contact management system as likely customers for any offers you make in the future.

Keep the work alive for yourself

When you lead or co-lead a no-cost *Overcoming Fear* program with a success team, book discussion group, or buddy, keep in mind that you are a participant yourself. So, the suggestions above for helping participants keep the work alive are ideas to consider adopting in your own life.

As a paid leader for *Overcoming Fear* programs, you might choose to lead a program each year or season. To position yourself as an ongoing resource for prospective participants, consider how you might incorporate themes related to the program into your regular marketing. You could write, speak, or post about any aspect of overcoming fear, resistance, and the inner critic to create a built-in audience for your programs each time you choose to offer one.

However you choose to incorporate the *Overcoming Fear* material into your business, career, or life, know that by leading this program, you'll be helping other self-employed professionals and creatives thrive. My hope is that you, my self-employed professional friend, will also be helping *yourself* thrive by doing so.

Appendix

Appendix Contents

Digital copies of the sample facilitation tools above are available for download at no cost. Visit chayden.com/ofsp-leaders for these.

Conducting a breakout exercise

With a group of four or fewer, breakout exercises typically won't be necessary, as you can have the full group participate in all activities. However, when you have five or more participants in a session, you likely won't have time for each person to participate with the whole group. You can break up your group into dyads of two or triads of three participants, and have them conduct the exercise in their smaller groups.

When meeting in person, this is easy to do by sending each group to a different part of the room or table. When meeting online, you can initiate breakout groups also, if your webinar platform license allows this capability. If you don't have the technical ability to host breakouts, you can substitute a fishbowl exercise instead (see below) and remind participants they'll have a chance to try the exercise on their own during skills practice in between sessions.

Be sure to give complete instructions for the exercise before starting to break up the group, so you'll keep their attention. Tell them how much time they'll have to complete the full exercise, and also how much time each person will have for their own portion. When possible, you can also choose to pop in and out of breakout groups to observe, and advise if needed.

You can ask breakout participants to debrief the exercise in their breakout groups, or request they hold off on debriefing until the full group is back together. Refer to *Guide* **Chapter Two** for appropriate debrief questions to use.

When participants are debriefing in their breakout groups, remind them about the guidelines for group debriefs that appear below.

Conducting a fishbowl exercise

In a fishbowl exercise, you select one person to be the "fish" and practice the skill to be learned, while the rest of the group forms the "bowl" observing. A fishbowl is typically followed by a group debrief. Ask for a volunteer to be the fish, or call on someone if no one steps up. When you have a choice of volunteers, choose the person who seems the most positive, so long as that person hasn't been the fish too recently.

Before beginning the exercise, ask the fish for their permission to work with them publicly on what may be a sensitive topic. Even when the fish has volunteered, this will create an additional feeling of safety. Ask the participants in the bowl to hold their reactions until your group debrief afterward.

Facilitating a group debrief

The purpose of a group debrief is to deepen everyone's learning about the skills being practiced, whether they practiced in between sessions or just then during the meeting. Most of a debrief should be spent on hearing from people how their skills practice went for them. Less time, if any, should be spent on what they noticed about another participant's practice.

While it's sometimes appropriate for observers to state their observations also, these must always be positive comments, rather than criticisms. For example, "I noticed how you projected more confidence when you smiled," is an appropriate observation. An inappropriate observation would be, "You seemed nervous before you started smiling."

Begin every debrief session by reminding participants of the above guidelines. Open the session by asking a specific question you want participants to answer, then let them know how you want them to respond. For example, will you call on each participant in turn? Or, will you ask for a couple of people to volunteer to speak? Or, will you conduct the debrief "popcorn" style, asking for brief responses from as many participants as possible, in turn, without waiting to be called on.

Appropriate debrief questions about participants' skills practice between or during sessions would be "How was it for you to practice XYZ?" or "What was it like for you to practice XYZ?" You could also ask "What did you experience when you practiced XYZ?" or "What did you learn from practicing XYZ?"

When debriefing the Practice Loop from *Book* **Chapter Two**, or identifying fears from *Book* **Chapter Four**, there are specific debrief questions which are recommended. You'll find those in the session-by-session facilitation outlines in *Guide* **Chapter Two**.

While a group debrief is in progress, keep the process moving by calling on additional participants or asking follow-up questions, as appropriate. Above all, maintain an atmosphere of curiosity and safety throughout. Debriefs must always encourage compassionate awareness, and never become occasions to voice criticism or negative judgments—of others or of oneself.

Sample public program promo page

Overcoming the Fear of Self-Promotion
with [Your Name]
Nine-Session Group Coaching Program
for Self-Employed Professionals and Creatives

[Day of Week], [Dates]
[Start Time]-[End Time] [Time Zone]

Learn to Vanquish Your Fear and Promote Yourself with
Confidence

Reluctance to promote yourself holds you back from achieving personal fulfillment and financial success. When you hesitate to broadcast your accomplishments and capabilities, your ideal clients never get a chance to find out what you can do for them. In this road-tested program, you will learn to overcome fear, resistance, and the inner critic, so you can promote yourself and your business confidently!

This powerful, insightful program, based on the book *Overcoming the Fear of Self-Promotion* by C.J. Hayden, has been taken by hundreds of self-employed professionals like you. In nine live, online lessons of 60 minutes each, followed by homework assignments, you will learn specific, actionable techniques for managing the fear and resistance you have about marketing and selling.

This program delivers step-by-step tools and techniques to overcome
fear and resistance to sales and marketing.

[Insert testimonial: For your first program, you may wish to use testimonials from your prior programs or coaching clients.]

Here's just some of what the program covers:

- How fear and resistance to sales and marketing works behind the scenes to sabotage you
- Step-by-step approaches to overcome the seven most common fears of self-promotion
- How to identify when fear, resistance, and your inner critic are running the show
- What you can do to reprogram your thinking about marketing and sales
- Specific techniques you can use to promote yourself even when it scares you
- How to transform your relationship with marketing, selling, and prospective clients so you can promote yourself confidently

With this program, you will loosen the grip of your fears and become a more courageous marketer.

[Insert testimonial]

Who this program is for:

- Consultants, coaches, and trainers
- Therapists, counselors, and health practitioners
- Financial advisors and brokers of insurance and real estate
- Writers, designers, and artists
- Fitness, lifestyle, and beauty professionals
- Self-employed professionals and freelancers
- Anyone who must promote their own services in order to succeed

This program will give you the boost you need to conquer the saboteurs getting in the way of your business success.

What you will learn:

- How to recognize fear or resistance in the moment, so you can get past it as it happens
- Discover your personal antidote to self-promotion fears
- What to do when fear masquerades as procrastination or avoidance
- Proven strategies for reprogramming your inner critic
- Quick fixes to use when fear or resistance shows up
- How to tell people about your capabilities without bragging or being pushy

[Insert testimonial]

Your program leader

[Your name] [Your photo]

[Insert 50-75 word bio]

About the program

We'll have nine one-hour learning sessions over a nine-week period, which will include discussion and time for questions. You'll have the opportunity to practice what you are learning in each session, as well as experiential homework that supports you to prepare and practice on your own. Enrollment will be limited to 10 people, so you'll get personal attention. Our sessions will be practical, interactive, and designed for skill-building.

We'll meet via Zoom so you can participate from anywhere. Each session will be recorded in case you need to miss one.

Please note: This program requires that you purchase a copy of *Overcoming the Fear of Self-Promotion* by C.J. Hayden, which will serve as our text. You can purchase the book as a paperback or ebook from any online bookseller or [Link to your preferred seller].

Complete nine-session program

[Your price]

[Registration link]

Questions about this program? Contact me! [Link to your contact info]

Sample in-house program promo page

Overcoming the Fear of Self-Promotion
with [Your Name]

Group Coaching Program
For Your Company's Employees, Students of Your School, or
Members of Your Organization

Help Them Learn to Vanquish Fear and Promote Themselves
with Confidence

Reluctance to promote themselves holds back your employees, students, or members from achieving personal fulfillment and financial success. When they hesitate to broadcast their accomplishments and capabilities, their ideal clients never get a chance to find out what they can do. In this road-tested program, they will learn to overcome fear, resistance, and the inner critic, so they can promote themselves and their business confidently!

This powerful, insightful program, based on the book *Overcoming the Fear of Self-Promotion* by C.J. Hayden, has been taken by hundreds of self-employed professionals and creatives like the ones you serve. In live, online lessons, followed by homework assignments, they will learn specific, actionable techniques for managing the fear and resistance they have about marketing and selling.

This program delivers step-by-step tools and techniques to overcome fear and resistance to sales and marketing.

[Insert testimonial: For your first program, you may wish to use testimonials from your prior programs, coaching clients, or speaking/training engagements.]

Here's just some of what the program covers:

- How fear and resistance to sales and marketing work behind the scenes as saboteurs
- Step-by-step approaches to overcome the seven most common fears of self-promotion
- How to identify when fear, resistance, and the inner critic are running the show
- What they can do to reprogram their thinking about marketing and sales
- Specific techniques they can use to promote themselves even when it scares them
- How to transform their relationship with marketing, selling, and prospective clients, so they can promote themselves confidently

With this program, your employees, students, or members will loosen the grip of their fears and become more courageous marketers.

[Insert testimonial]

Who this program is for:

- Consultants, coaches, and trainers
- Therapists, counselors, and health practitioners
- Financial advisors and brokers of insurance and real estate
- Writers, designers, and artists
- Fitness, lifestyle, and beauty professionals
- Self-employed professionals and freelancers
- Anyone who must promote their own services in order to succeed

This program will give your employees, students, or members the boost they need to conquer saboteurs getting in the way of their business success.

What participants will learn:

- How to recognize fear or resistance in the moment, so they can get past it as it happens
- Discover their personal antidote to self-promotion fears
- What to do when fear masquerades as procrastination or avoidance
- Proven strategies for reprogramming their inner critic
- Quick fixes to use when fear or resistance shows up
- How to tell people about their capabilities without bragging or being pushy

[Insert testimonial]

About the program leader

[Your name] [Your photo]

[Insert 50-75 word bio]

About the program

This program is available in the following formats:

- Nine-session series, meeting weekly for 60 minutes
- Five-session series, meeting biweekly or monthly for 90 minutes

Each learning session includes discussion and time for questions. Participants will have the opportunity to practice what they are learning in each session, as well as receiving experiential homework that supports them to prepare and practice on their own. A maximum of 10 people can be accommodated in each program, so all participants will get personal attention. The learning sessions will be practical, interactive, and designed for skill-building.

All programs meet via Zoom so your group can participate from anywhere. Each session will be recorded in case anyone needs to miss one.

To find out more about how you can bring this trusted, effective program to your organization, contact me at [Your contact information and/or link to it].

Sample book group/success team promo page/email copy

Want to Join a Success Team for Self-Employed Professionals?

Would you like to work through the book *Overcoming the Fear of Self-Promotion* [Link to an online bookseller or the book description on the cjhayden.com site] by C.J. Hayden with me and a small group of self-employed professionals? I'm seeking 3-5 people to join me for a group beginning in [Month] [Year]. The only cost would be buying yourself a copy of the book.

The book lays out a complete program for learning to manage your fear and resistance about marketing and selling. Each chapter teaches specific, actionable techniques, and concludes with skills practice assignments. These are some of the topics the book covers:

- Step-by-step approaches to overcome the seven most common fears of self-promotion
- What you can do to transform your thinking about marketing and sales
- How to recognize fear or resistance in the moment, so you can get past it as it happens
- Proven strategies for reprogramming your inner critic
- Quick fixes to use when fear or resistance shows up
- How to tell people about your capabilities without bragging or being pushy

The book was written specifically for self-employed professionals and creatives. Here are examples of professions that have found it helpful:

- Consultants, coaches, and trainers
- Therapists, counselors, and health practitioners
- Financial advisors and brokers of insurance and real estate

- Writers, designers, and artists
- Fitness, lifestyle, and beauty professionals
- Self-employed professionals and freelancers
- Anyone who must promote their own services in order to succeed

Here's some info about me so you can see if we might enjoy working together:

[Your bio]

I'm picturing we'll meet for a total of 9 one-hour sessions, one per week, at a time agreeable to everyone. We'll meet via Zoom so we can participate from wherever we are, and I'll facilitate the sessions. You'll need to purchase a copy of the book, which you can get as a paperback or ebook from any online bookseller or [Link to your preferred seller]. There's no other cost involved.

If you're interested or have questions, please email me at [Your email address or link to a contact page] or text me at [Your mobile number] before [Date]. Please let me know a little about yourself when you get in touch.

Sample individual coaching program promo page

Overcoming the Fear of Self-Promotion
with [Your Name]
One-on-One Coaching Program
for Self-Employed Professionals

Learn to Vanquish Your Fear and Promote Yourself with Confidence

Reluctance to promote yourself holds you back from achieving personal fulfillment and financial success. When you hesitate to broadcast your accomplishments and capabilities, your ideal clients never get a chance to find out what you can do for them. With this road-tested coaching program and me as your coach, you will learn to overcome fear, resistance, and the inner critic, so you can promote yourself and your business confidently!

This powerful, insightful program, based on the book *Overcoming the Fear of Self-Promotion* by C.J. Hayden, has helped hundreds of self-employed professionals like you. In nine individual Zoom sessions of 60 minutes each, followed by homework assignments, you will learn and practice specific, actionable techniques for managing the fear and resistance you have about marketing and selling.

[Insert testimonial: For your first client, you may wish to use testimonials from any prior programs or coaching clients.]

Here's just some of what you'll learn from our sessions:
- How fear and resistance to sales and marketing works behind the scenes to sabotage you
- Step-by-step approaches to overcome the seven most common fears of self-promotion

- How to identify when fear, resistance, and your inner critic are running the show
- What you can do to reprogram your thinking about marketing and sales
- Specific techniques you can use to promote yourself even when it scares you
- How to transform your relationship with marketing, selling, and prospective clients so you can promote yourself confidently

Working with me and this program, you will loosen the grip of your fears and become a more courageous marketer.

[Insert testimonial]

Who this coaching program is for:
- Consultants, coaches, and trainers
- Therapists, counselors, and health practitioners
- Financial advisors and brokers of insurance and real estate
- Writers, designers, and artists
- Fitness, lifestyle, and beauty professionals
- Self-employed professionals and freelancers
- Anyone who must promote their own services in order to succeed

The tools and techniques of this program will give you the boost you need to conquer the saboteurs getting in the way of your business success.

What you will learn:
- How to recognize fear or resistance in the moment, so you can get past it as it happens
- Discover your personal antidote to self-promotion fears
- What to do when fear masquerades as procrastination or avoidance

- Proven strategies for reprogramming your inner critic
- Quick fixes to use when fear or resistance shows up
- How to tell people about your capabilities without bragging or being pushy

[Insert testimonial]

Your coach for this program

[Your name] [Your photo]

[Insert 50-75 word bio]

About the coaching program

We'll schedule nine 60-minute one-on-one coaching sessions over a nine-week period. You'll have the opportunity to practice what you are learning with me in each session, as well as experiential homework that supports you to prepare and practice on your own.

We'll meet via Zoom so you can participate from anywhere. Our sessions will be practical, interactive, and designed for skill-building.

Please note: This program requires that you purchase a copy of *Overcoming the Fear of Self-Promotion* by C.J. Hayden, which will serve as our text. You can purchase the book as a paperback or ebook from any online bookseller or [Link to your preferred seller].

Complete nine-session program

[Your price]

[Enrollment link]

Questions about this program? Contact me! [Link to your contact info]

Sample invitation email for a public program

Subject: Join me next month to overcome your fear of self-promotion

Hello, [First name]!

Are you sometimes reluctant to promote yourself? When you hesitate to broadcast your accomplishments and capabilities, your ideal clients never get a chance to find out what you can do for them. Beginning [Start date], I'm offering a road-tested program where you will learn to overcome fear, resistance, and the inner critic, so you can promote yourself and your business confidently!

This powerful, insightful program, based on the book *Overcoming the Fear of Self-Promotion* by C.J. Hayden, has been taken by hundreds of self-employed professionals like you. In nine live, online lessons of 60 minutes each, followed by homework assignments, you will learn specific, actionable techniques for managing the fear and resistance you have about marketing and selling.

[Insert testimonial: For your first program, you may wish to use testimonials from your prior programs or coaching clients.]

Here's just some of what the program covers:

- Step-by-step approaches to overcome the seven most common fears of self-promotion
- What you can do to transform your thinking about marketing and sales
- How to recognize fear or resistance in the moment, so you can get past it as it happens
- Proven strategies for reprogramming your inner critic

- Quick fixes to use when fear or resistance shows up
- How to tell people about your capabilities without bragging or being pushy

[Insert testimonial]

Who this program is for:
- Consultants, coaches, and trainers
- Therapists, counselors, and health practitioners
- Financial advisors and brokers of insurance and real estate
- Writers, designers, and artists
- Fitness, lifestyle, and beauty professionals
- Self-employed professionals and freelancers
- Anyone who must promote their own services in order to succeed

We'll have nine one-hour learning sessions over a nine-week period, which will include discussion and time for questions. You'll have the opportunity to practice what you are learning in each session, as well as experiential homework that supports you to prepare and practice on your own. Enrollment will be limited to 10 people, so you'll get personal attention.

We'll meet via Zoom so you can participate from anywhere. Each session will be recorded in case you need to miss one.

[Insert testimonial]

Interested? Find out more here: [Registration link]

Questions? Just hit reply or call/text [Phone number]

Sample invitation email for an in-house program

Subject: I'd like to help your [employees/students/members] get more clients

[First name], at [target organization's name], your success can depend on the success of your [employees/students/members] at building a client base. But reluctance to promote themselves can hold them back. When they hesitate to broadcast their accomplishments and capabilities, their ideal clients never get a chance to find out what they can do.

I offer a road-tested training and coaching program called *Overcoming the Fear of Self-Promotion*. It's specifically designed for self-employed professionals and creatives like the [Insert name of profession served by the organization, e.g. therapists, stylists, or coaches] your organization [employs/trains/serves].

This powerful, insightful program, based on the book by C.J. Hayden, has been taken by hundreds of self-employed professionals. In live, online lessons, followed by homework assignments, your [employees/students/members] will learn specific, actionable techniques for managing the fear and resistance they have about marketing and selling.

[Insert testimonial: For your first program, you may wish to use testimonials from your prior programs, coaching clients, or speaking/training engagements.]

Here's just some of what the program covers:

- How fear and resistance to sales and marketing work behind the scenes as saboteurs

- Step-by-step approaches to overcome the seven most common fears of self-promotion
- How to identify when fear, resistance, and the inner critic are running the show
- What they can do to reprogram their thinking about marketing and sales
- Specific techniques they can use to promote themselves even when it scares them
- How to transform their relationship with marketing, selling, and prospective clients, so they can promote themselves confidently

With this program, your [employees/students/members] will loosen the grip of their fears and become more courageous marketers.

[Insert testimonial]

I'm [your name], [Insert 50-75 word bio]

This program is available in the following formats:

- Nine-session series, meeting weekly for 60 minutes
- Five-session series, meeting biweekly or monthly for 90 minutes

Each learning session includes discussion and time for questions. Participants will have the opportunity to practice what they are learning in each session, as well as receiving experiential homework that supports them to prepare and practice on their own. A maximum of 10 people can be accommodated in each program, so all participants will get personal attention.

All programs meet via Zoom so your group can participate from anywhere. Each session will be recorded in case anyone needs to miss one.

Various pricing models are available, depending on how your organization typically works with contract trainers and coaches like myself.

To find out more about how you can bring this trusted, effective program to your organization, contact me at [your contact information].

Sample business proposal for an in-house program

Overcoming the Fear of Self-Promotion
Nine-Session Training and Coaching Program
for [Organization name]
From [Your name]
[Your title or company name]

[Date]

Dear [first name]:

I am pleased to have this opportunity to propose a training and coaching program for the [employees/students/members] of [organization name]. Following is an outline of the content, structure, and pricing for the program I'm proposing. I look forward to discussing this with you, and will be in touch soon.

CONTENTS
I.   Overcoming the Fear of Self-Promotion Program Overview
II. Program Leader and Logistics
III. Participant Requirements
IV. Program Fees

Warmly,
[Your name]

I.   Overcoming the Fear of Self-Promotion Program Overview

Overcoming the Fear of Self-Promotion is a training and coaching program series delivered to hundreds of self-employed professionals and creatives worldwide since 1994. It was designed specifically for this audience to help them overcome the fear, resistance, and inner critic voice that holds them back from marketing and sales success. Unlike other similar programs, *Overcoming Fear* is based on research conducted by psychologists and neuroscientists, as well as decades of experience and training in life and business coaching.

The program delivers training and coaching combined, delivered by a seasoned facilitator. Each session in the series includes pre-class reading, learning points delivered by lecture, experiential exercises, and homework assignments. Participants receive constructive feedback from both the facilitator and their fellow participants.

Overcoming Fear teaches specific, actionable techniques to help participants break through their self-imposed limitations on marketing and selling. Program participants learn new approaches, develop new skills, and reprogram negative behaviors and beliefs. The program textbook includes 120 pages of tools, tactics, examples, and exercises.

Participants learn the following, and much more:

- How fear and resistance to sales and marketing work behind the scenes as saboteurs
- Step-by-step approaches to overcome the seven most common fears of self-promotion
- How to identify when fear, resistance, and the inner critic are running the show
- What they can do to reprogram their thinking about marketing and sales
- Specific techniques they can use to promote themselves even when it scares them
- How to transform their relationship with marketing, selling, and prospective clients, so they can promote themselves confidently

Program structure and agenda:

The program will be delivered as a nine-session series via Zoom, meeting weekly for 60 minutes, for a total of nine hours class time.

Each session includes discussion and time for questions. Participants will have the opportunity to practice what they are learning, as well as receiving experiential homework assignments that support them to prepare and practice on their own.

Session 1: Introduction—Learning to Manage Fear & the IAAM Technique

- Welcome to the program
- What fear of marketing and sales is about and where it comes from
- What to expect as you begin learning to manage your fear
- How to use the I AAM Technique
- Why and how the I AAM Technique works
- Examples and real-life experience with the technique

Session 2: Building Your Fear-Defeating Muscles with the Practice Loop

- The impact of raising awareness about your fear and resistance
- How to use the Practice Loop approach
- Live demo of the Practice Loop
- How to debrief when using the Practice Loop
- When fear masquerades as resistance, procrastination, or avoidance
- Examples and real-life experience with the Practice Loop

Session 3: Taming Your Inner Critic

- What the inner critic voice is and where it comes from
- The impact of the inner critic on your marketing
- Steps for managing the inner critic

- Using disputation as a management technique
- Live examples of how to manage your critic
- Tips and tricks to overcome your inner critic in the moment

Session 4: Identifying Your Self-Promotion Fears

- Why there is value in identifying your fear
- Seven distinct fears of self-promotion
- How to identify your primary fear
- Digging deeper to identify fear if needed
- Thoughts and realizations about how fear works

Session 5: Finding Your Personal Fear Antidote

- Why you need to stop denying or resisting fear
- What role fear plays in keeping you safe
- How to manage your fear by making friends with it
- Positive qualities you can develop to manage fear
- How to approach retraining your reptilian brain
- Identifying your personal antidote to fear

Session 6: Developing Your Fear Antidote

- How to build the positive qualities that will reassure your fear
- Seven specific strategies for building positive qualities
- Evidence and examples of these quality-building strategies at work
- Four extra strategies to build positive qualities

Session 7: Quick Fixes for Fearful Moments

- How to develop long-term solutions for fear
- Why you need both long-term solutions and quick fixes
- Five quick fixes to use in fearful moments
- Live examples of using quick fixes

Session 8: Defeating Fear with Stronger Relationships

- How and why stronger relationships will help you overcome fear
- How to build stronger relationships with prospective clients
- How to build relationships with other professionals
- Where and how to connect with people and get to know them

Session 9: Wrap-up—Putting It All Together

- How to combine all the techniques of this program to manage fear
- Six-step system for ongoing fear management
- Practicing fear management as a long-term strategy

II. Program Leader and Logistics

The program will be delivered by [your name].

[Insert 50-75 word bio]

The program requires a minimum of 4 participants and can accommodate a maximum of 10 participants, so all participants will get personal attention. All sessions will be delivered live via the program leader's Zoom platform. Sessions will be recorded in case anyone needs to miss one.

In addition to the live sessions, the program recommends that each participant practice the skills being learned with a buddy each week. The program leader will assist participants in setting up these buddy practice sessions.

III. Participant Requirements

- Each participant must have their own copy of the book *Overcoming the Fear of Self-Promotion* by C.J. Hayden
- Availability to attend the majority of class sessions
- Ability to spend 1-2 additional hours per week for study and practice of the tools and skills being taught
- Proficiency in spoken and written English

IV.   Program Fees

[Vary the text below based on the type of organization and participants]

[For flat fee arrangements]

The program for [organization name] will be a private program, offered at a flat fee of [your price] for a minimum of 4 participants and a maximum of 10 participants. A deposit of 50% is required to reserve the program dates, with the balance due on the day the program begins.

[For per person arrangements]

The program for [organization name] will be a private program, offered at the fee per participant of [your price]. You are free to offer this program to your [students/members] at any price you wish. The recommended price is [your price x 2], to establish a 50/50 split of revenue between [organization name] and the program leader.

A minimum of 4 participants will be required for the program to go forward. The program will accommodate a maximum of 10 participants. A deposit of [your price x 2] will be required to reserve the program dates, with the balance due on the day the program begins.

Sample letter of agreement for an in-house program

Please note: If you use this sample as a model, you will be doing so at your own risk. I can't offer you any guarantees that this document will protect your rights under all circumstances and in all locations.

[Date]

[Client name]

[Client address]

Dear [client name]:

Thank you for asking me to deliver my program for [organization name]'s [employees/students/members]. To assist us in organizing a successful program together, this letter will confirm our agreement and outline special requirements.

Topic: Overcoming the Fear of Self-Promotion

Program Leader: [Your name]

Dates/Times: [Day of week], [start date] to [end date], [time] [time zone]

Location: Zoom platform provided by program leader

Fee [for flat fee arrangements]: [Your price] for up to 10 participants

Fee [for per person arrangements]: [Your price] per person for a minimum of 4 participants and a maximum of 10 participants

DEPOSIT: To guarantee these dates, please send a deposit of [your required amount] with a signed copy of this letter within ten days. Please make your check payable to [your company name], or pay online as shown on the attached invoice.

CANCELLATION SCHEDULE: As a cancellation can cause an irreplaceable loss of income, it is necessary to include the following cancellation schedule.

[For flat fee arrangements]

Notice of Cancellation	Balance Due of Total Fee
91 or more days	0% (your deposit will be refunded)
61-90 days	25% (1/2 of your deposit will be refunded)
31-60 days	50% (your deposit will not be refunded)
11-30 days	75% (you will owe an additional 25% of fee)
Less than 10 days	100% (you will owe the remaining 50% of the minimum fee)

[For per person arrangements]

If the minimum enrollment of 4 participants is not met by 10 days before the program start date, the program will be cancelled, and your deposit will not be refunded. If the program is cancelled for any other reason, the following schedule applies.

Notice of Cancellation	Balance Due
91 or more days	Your deposit will be refunded
31-90 days	1/2 of your deposit will be refunded
10-30 days	Your deposit will not be refunded
Less than 10 days	You will owe an additional amount equal to the original deposit

REFUND POLICY [For per-person arrangements]: Because this program has limited enrollment, no refunds will be granted if a participant's situation changes after the program begins.

FORCE MAJEURE: If the program leader is prevented from delivering your program on the scheduled dates by any circumstances beyond either party's control, including weather conditions, civil emergency, labor dispute, accident, illness, or act of God, both parties will make a good faith attempt to reschedule the program. If the parties cannot agree on a new program schedule, this agreement will be cancelled and neither party will have any liability for expenses or losses incurred. If the program leader must cancel for one of the above reasons, they will attempt to provide a comparable leader acceptable to you, and if no substitute leader is possible, your deposit will be refunded.

FINAL PAYMENT: The balance due of the fee will be payable on the program start date. Please have a check mailed to arrive by that date, or pay online as shown on the attached invoice.

REQUIRED TEXTBOOK: Each participant must possess their own copy of *Overcoming the Fear of Self-Promotion* by C.J. Hayden. The text may be purchased by your organization or the participants themselves. The book is available in paperback and multiple ebook formats at most online booksellers, and cjhayden.com.

REGISTRATION: Your organization will be responsible for registering participants in this program, and for collecting any fees due from participants. Be sure to alert participants to the textbook requirement to give them sufficient time to acquire the book before the program. You will provide the program leader with a final list of participant names, email addresses, and phone numbers no later than five business days before the program begins. You are also welcome to provide participant names as each participant registers.

AUDIO/VIDEO RECORDING: Audio or video recording of my program by your organization is not permitted. I will provide session recordings for the use of paid participants only, to assist them in catching up if they miss a session. These recordings remain my property, and neither participants nor your organization will have long-term access to them.

Thank you for giving me the opportunity to work with your organization. I look forward to delivering a successful program, and to a mutually rewarding relationship between us. If you have any questions or need additional information, please call or email me.

Sincerely,

[Your name]

Accepted for Client

Signature:

Date:

Name:

Title:

Sample welcome email for a public group program (adapt as needed for in-house programs or individual clients)

Subject: Welcome to Overcoming the Fear of Self-Promotion

[First name], I'm pleased to welcome you to the training and coaching program *Overcoming the Fear of Self-Promotion*. My name is [your name] and I will be your program leader. I am looking forward to working with you! Please read this email carefully and keep it for your future reference.

The program will take place via Zoom on [day of week] from [start date] to [end date] from [start time] to [end time] [time zone].

ACCESS DETAILS FOR ALL MEETINGS

[Your Zoom link]

Meeting ID: [Your Zoom meeting ID]

Password: [Your Zoom password]

Please add the program dates, times, and access details to your calendar now. If you know you will miss a session or arrive late, please let me know at [your email].

REQUIRED TEXTBOOK

To participate in this program, you must possess a copy of *Overcoming the Fear of Self-Promotion* by C.J. Hayden. The book is available in paperback and multiple ebook formats at most online booksellers, and cjhayden.com.

Before our first session, please read these sections of the book: "What to Know Before You Begin" and "Chapter One: You Can Learn to Manage Fear."

PROGRAM MATERIALS

You will need to download these three PDFs for the program:

- Program syllabus [link], which includes ground rules for the program, our session schedule, list of required reading, and suggested skills practice between sessions
- Roster of all participants [link]
- Practice pal assignments [link] [If you're offering this option]

Please have the syllabus and the book available during our sessions, as we'll be referring to them. You may also wish to have available your preferred way to take notes.

REFUND POLICY

Your enrollment fee is fully refundable up to 72 hours before the program begins. If you must cancel after that, please send a friend in your place. Because this program has limited enrollment, no refunds will be granted if your situation changes after you begin the program. However, if you are dissatisfied in any way, your program fee will be fully refundable.

Please contact me at [your email] or [your phone] if you have any questions. Talk to you soon!

Warmly,

[Your name]

Sample program syllabus

OVERCOMING THE FEAR OF SELF-PROMOTION PROGRAM
SYLLABUS

PROGRAM GROUND RULES

To make this program productive and enjoyable for all participants,
please observe the following ground rules.

1. Make your best effort to arrive on time for each session and plan
   to stay for the entire time.
2. If you know you will miss or arrive late to a session, please
   email me at [your email].
3. Participate from a location where you won't be interrupted or
   distracted. Do not join a session while you are driving.
4. Leave your camera on so we can all see each other.
5. If there is background noise in your area, mute your mic except
   when you are speaking.
6. Keep confidential whatever you learn about other participants.
   You are welcome to discuss your own learning and experience
   in the program, but no one else's.
7. Allow everyone a chance to talk, and be sure to speak up
   yourself.
8. Ask questions during class sessions when time permits. If you
   have questions between sessions, email me at [your email].
9. Everyone's viewpoint is valuable, and everyone's experience is
   valid. Except when you are invited to provide structured
   feedback, make only positive comments to other participants,
   and refrain from criticizing or invalidating others.
10. Maintain a mindset of compassionate awareness about your
    own emotions, beliefs, and performance regarding self-
    promotion.

ACCESS DETAILS FOR ALL MEETINGS

[Your Zoom link]

Meeting ID: [Your Zoom meeting ID]

Password: [Your Zoom password]

PROGRAM SCHEDULE & OUTLINE

[Day of week] from [start date] to [end date] from [start time] to [end time] [time zone].

[For nine-session series]

[Date] Session 1 – Introduction: Learning to Manage Fear & the IAAM Technique

Pre-session reading:

- What to Know Before You Begin
- Chapter One: You Can Learn to Manage Fear

Post-session skills practice:

- Try the IAAM Technique

[Date] Session 2 – Building Your Fear-Defeating Muscles & the Practice Loop

Pre-session reading:

- Chapter Two: Building Your Fear-Defeating Muscles

Post-session skills practice:

- Make use of the Practice Loop

[Date] Session 3 – Taming Your Inner Critic & Disputation

Pre-session reading:

- Chapter Three: Taming Your Inner Critic

Post-session skills practice:

- Manage your inner critic with disputation and quick tricks

[Date] Session 4 – Identifying Your Self-Promotion Fears

Pre-session reading:

- Chapter Four: Identifying Your Self-Promotion Fears

Post-session skills practice:

- Practice self-promotion
- Identify your fear

[Date] Session 5 – Finding Your Personal Fear Antidote

Pre-session reading:

- Chapter Five: Finding Your Personal Fear Antidote

Post-session skills practice:

- Discover your best fear antidote

[Date] Session 6 – Developing Your Fear Antidote

Pre-session reading:

- Chapter Six: Developing Your Fear Antidote

Post-session skills practice:

- Try on a strategy to develop your fear antidote

[Date] Session 7 – Quick Fixes for Fearful Moments

Pre-session reading:

- Chapter Seven: Quick Fixes for Fearful Moments

Post-session skills practice:

- Continue building your fear antidote
- Add a quick fix

[Date] Session 8 – Defeating Fear with Stronger Relationships

Pre-session reading:

- Chapter Eight: Defeating Fear with Stronger Relationships

Post-session skills practice:

- Begin to build more relationships
- Outline your personal fear management plan

[Date] Session 9 – Wrap-up: Putting It All Together

Pre-session reading:

- What to Do When You Finish this Book

[For five-session series]

[Date] Session 1 – Introduction: Learning to Manage Fear & the IAAM Technique

Pre-session reading:

- What to Know Before You Begin
- Chapter One: You Can Learn to Manage Fear

Post-session skills practice:

- Try the IAAM Technique

[Date] Session 2 – Building Your Fear-Defeating Muscles & Taming Your Inner Critic

Pre-session reading:

- Chapter Two: Building Your Fear-Defeating Muscles
- Chapter Three: Taming Your Inner Critic

Post-session skills practice:

- Make use of the Practice Loop
- Manage your inner critic with disputation and quick tricks

[Date] Session 3 – Identifying Your Self-Promotion Fears & Finding Your Personal Fear Antidote

Pre-session reading:

- Chapter Four: Identifying Your Self-Promotion Fears
- Chapter Five: Finding Your Personal Fear Antidote

Post-session skills practice:

- Practice self-promotion
- Identify your fear
- Discover your best fear antidote

[Date] Session 4 – Developing Your Fear Antidote & Quick Fixes for Fearful Moments

Pre-session reading:

- Chapter Six: Developing Your Fear Antidote
- Chapter Seven: Quick Fixes for Fearful Moments

Post-session skills practice:

- Try on a strategy to develop your fear antidote
- Add a quick fix

[Date] Session 5 – Wrap-up: Defeating Fear with Stronger Relationships & Putting It All Together

Pre-session reading:

- Chapter Eight: Defeating Fear with Stronger Relationships
- What to Do When You Finish this Book

WORKING WITH A PRACTICE PAL [If you're offering this option]

Meeting with a practice pal between program sessions will make it easier for you to complete the skills practice you'll be doing as homework, plus furnish you with additional accountability outside of class.

I've provided you with a participant roster for our program, and a table of practice pal assignments. You'll be rotating pals for each practice session, so you'll gain experience working with different people. Please reach out to all your assigned practice pals for the entire program immediately after our first session, to coordinate a 30- to 45-minute practice time between each session. Duos should need only 30 minutes; trios may need 45 minutes.

Locking in your practice schedule for the entire program during the first week is the best approach to make sure that all practice sessions happen. If you happen to miss a class session, you should still attend the following practice session whenever possible.

In each practice, have each pal take a turn at practicing the homework given for the previous session. For example, after Session 1, you would practice using the IAAM Technique from Chapter One in the book.

While a practice pal is speaking, the other pal(s) should listen carefully and note what they hear. First, they should ask the speaker to debrief their own experience, structured this way:

- What worked about what you did, what you said, or how you were?
- What didn't work about it?
- What did you notice about what you thought, felt emotionally, or felt physically?
- What do you want to do or say differently, or how do you want to be different next time?

Then the listening pal(s) should provide their own feedback using the "sandwich" approach, structured like this:

1. What I thought worked well was…
2. What I thought didn't work as well was…
3. What I appreciated was…

For example, a practice pal listening to someone's practice of the I AAM Technique might say:

1. I thought you did an excellent job of noticing what was going on with you about that thing.
2. What didn't work as well was that you didn't seem to accept everything you were noticing.
3. What I appreciated was your willingness to look honestly at this uncomfortable stuff.

Remember that everything you learn from another participant is confidential. Anything revealed by pals in practice sessions should not be discussed with others not enrolled in the program.

Emergency enrollment measures

If your program or group has low or no registrations as the planned start date approaches, the following ideas can help you increase enrollment.

- Call everyone on your prospect list and invite them personally. Don't count on email and social media to do the job. Place a phone call to each person you have a phone number for, give a brief description of the program, and invite them to attend. You'll be amazed how many people will say, "Thank you for calling—I've been meaning to sign up." For an in-house program, ask the sponsor if they are willing to make some phone calls.
- Ask your clients and colleagues to make referrals. Just emailing an announcement to potential referral sources isn't the same as personally asking for their help. Call or email people who respect your work, and ask if they know two or three people who could benefit. If they have suggestions for you, ask if they are willing to contact those people themselves to endorse your program.
- Make a special offer. Tell the participants who are already registered they can bring a friend for half-price. You're not losing any revenue that way if the space would otherwise be standing empty. Or, offer a low-cost bonus gift to those who enroll—30 minutes of your professional time, or an ebook, audio/video, or report you've produced. To encourage people to spread the word, offer the same gift to people who refer students to you. Ask your contacts to share your offer with their own mailing list. Post about your offer on social media also.
- Attend in-person networking events that permit announcements or flyers about upcoming events.
- Post program invitations to online groups that permit self-promotion. Some groups allow this only on one day per week or per month.

In the last few days before your start date, if you still have only a handful registered:

- Instead of canceling your program, give yourself more time for enrollment by rescheduling for a later date. Implement any additional marketing ideas from *Guide* **Chapters Three, Four, or Five** you didn't previously try, as well as the ideas above.

- Or, hold your program on the planned date regardless of low enrollment. Invite people to enroll for free if necessary to have good participation, or ask your program's sponsor to do this. Your existing clients will enjoy the chance to spend more time with you; your colleagues will benefit from seeing you work and meeting other participants. Ask those who enroll at no charge to write glowing testimonials and refer paying participants for next time.

- If you can't fix it, feature it. The meaning of this classic sales maxim is that if your product has an obvious flaw, make it a positive selling point. When only four people enroll in your program, position it as an intimate group experience. If you have only two people in your group, describe it as a success team. Your participants will be thrilled to have more individual attention. There's no need to apologize for fewer-than-expected participants.

- Plan ahead to do better next time. Analyze what went wrong with your marketing, or your sponsor's marketing, and strategize how to do it differently next time around. Should you have allowed more lead time? Does your mailing list need to be larger? Do you need to factor in more promotion channels instead of relying on emails? Did your sponsor fail to follow through on their promised marketing? Make a list of all the key elements you think are necessary to successfully promote your next program.

Filling public group programs becomes easier when you offer them regularly. When students see the same program promoted two or three times, they are much more likely to enroll. Think of all your marketing efforts as part of a long-term plan to make more potential clients aware of your offers. If the outreach for your program introduces your services to many new people, you may ultimately find that much more valuable than just filling one program.

Sample participant's fear management plan

"I plan to use the six steps for fear management each time I find myself fearful or resistant about self-promotion, paying particular attention to disputing my inner critic, 'The Schoolmarm,' and overcoming my fear of disapproval. I'm going to spend four hours per month working on building relationships with potential clients and my colleagues. And, I'm going to continue building my fear antidote of self-sufficiency by granting myself a special permission at the beginning of every work day. "

About the Author

C.J. Hayden is a business coach, writing mentor, and the author of seven other books, including the bestselling *Get Clients Now! A 28-Day Marketing Program for Professionals, Consultants and Coaches*. The *Get Clients Now!* book is now in its third edition, and has been translated into multiple languages. Thousands of self-employed professionals and creatives around the world have made *Get Clients Now!* their sales and marketing bible.

Since 1992, C.J. has coached and trained self-employed professionals to get clients, get strategic, and get their writing done. She has over 40 years of business management experience, holds the credential Certified Professional Co-Active Coach, and completed advanced coach training with the Coaches Training Institute and Arbinger Institute.

In addition to her books, C.J. has written hundreds of blog posts and articles on marketing, entrepreneurship, and nonfiction writing. She hosts monthly Get It Written Days and an online community for self-employed professionals and creatives who write.

A popular speaker and workshop leader, C.J. has presented hundreds of programs to international audiences, and taught classes for John F. Kennedy University, Mills College, and the U.S. Small Business Administration.

To find out more about C.J.'s books and home-study courses, or to schedule an interview, visit cjhayden.com.

Did you find this book valuable? Your brief review will help spread the word. Please take a moment to leave a review with your favorite bookseller or review site. Thank you! I appreciate your support.

www.ingramcontent.com/pod-product-compliance
Lightning Source LLC
Chambersburg PA
CBHW060603200326
41521CB00007B/650